AF333335

# KENT VILLAGES

# *Kent Villages*

ALAN BIGNELL

ROBERT HALE · LONDON

# Contents

# Illustrations

PICTURE CREDITS

*Kentish Express:* 18, 19, 50; *Kent Messenger:* 2, 3, 4, 6, 7, 9, 12, 14, 15, 16, 17, 20, 25, 26, 27, 28, 30, 31, 32, 33, 34, 35, 36, 37, 38, 39, 40, 41, 42, 43, 44, 45, 46, 47, 52; Richard Rideout: 1, 5, 8, 10, 11, 13, 21, 22, 23, 24, 29, 48, 49, 51, 53, 54.

# I

## *Divided Garden*

WHEN it comes to swapping stories of past glories, Kent can hold its own with any county in England. If the talk is of history made in the heat of battle, or of events set in train by the strength of character of a single man; of poets or orators, artists or artisans; of philosophers, farmers, divines or eccentrics—make no mistake, Kent can match biographies with the best of them. Should the topic turn to places of interest, or of spectacular scenery, Kent can be condescending in the company of almost all England. And were the conversation of the counties to take a doleful turn towards claims of where the biggest changes are taking place today, then Kent can cap the experiences of most of its fellows on that subject, too.

The 1974 reorganization of local government made Kent the largest of the county administrations. It is the most heavily populated, and it plays host to more of the travelling public, particularly through its Channel Ports of Dover and Folkestone, than any other county in Britain. Tourism in Kent is a £100 million a year industry now, and growing.

Anyone who takes the blossom tour trail, which the motoring organizations blaze with direction signs each spring, cannot doubt that this is still the Garden of England, indeed, where the two principal fruit growing areas of the county, along the North Downs, and in Mid-Kent from Maidstone south to the Sussex border, together produce nearly half the country's apples and practically all its cherries—as well as rather more than half of Britain's total hop crop.

More than one-eighth of all Kent's 900,000-plus acres are woodland. The Forestry Commission is responsible for about 12,000 acres, but most of the rest is made up of comparatively small, scattered and privately-owned woods and coppices. They are not there simply to embellish the Kent countryside, however well they do just that. A great deal of the county's woodland includes some of the best sweet chestnut coppices in Britain, grown as a crop every bit as important to the county's overall agricultural pattern as the fruit, the hops and the other farm crops. It is not the nuts that are the commercially important crop, but the wood of the trees themselves, which are cropped for fencing and hop poles, and then allowed to grow again for another twelve or fifteen years before they are ready for the next harvest.

Oh, yes, Kent has plenty to congratulate itself upon. But it has its problems, too, like anywhere else. It is, for instance, a divided county. Since ancient times, it has allowed its river Medway to separate the Men of Kent on the eastern bank from the Kentish Men in the west, and not all the cross-currents of modern travel habits, nor the changes that are taking place in villages and towns on both sides of the river have yet totally obscured the differences between the two.

But much more important for the development of the county has been the division created by the hulking sweep of the North Downs, which curve in a great east-west arc with scarcely a break, and divide the north of the county from the south. It is this great natural barrier that has dictated the routes that are taken by the county's main road and rail lines. These, in turn, emphasize Kent's role as a corridor of communication between the capital and the Continent.

On the north side of the Downs, the A2 follows generally the line of the old Roman Watling Street all the way between London and Dover. Southwards, it is the A20 which links London with

Folkestone. Both are reminders of that much, much older route between the two of them, the pre-historic North Downs Way which is picturesquely, but for the most part inaccurately, known as the Pilgrim's Way.

The railway lines tend to repeat the same pattern, using the natural gaps of the Darent, Medway and Stour valleys to link the old London, Chatham and Dover Railway lines of North Kent with the former South-Eastern Railway line, the spinal column of the South Kent rail system which runs for forty-five miles from Redhill in Surrey to Ashford in Kent in an almost perfectly straight and level line before curving away towards Hythe and Folkestone.

It is a fact that all the north-south lines of communication across Kent are comparatively poor. The only two motorways of which the county can boast are mere improvements of the existing A2 and A20 routes, the most recent of a long succession of improvements to these two main roads through the county. Today, it is possible to travel the sixty miles or so from the Kent coast to London by train in about a couple of hours. Thousands of commuters do it every day. It takes longer to cross Kent by train from, say, Herne Bay to Tunbridge Wells by the most direct route via Canterbury, Ashford and Tonbridge, with changes at each of those stations. As the crow flies, it is about thirty-five miles. As the car travels on narrow, winding minor roads, it is at least twice as far. A north-south journey across Kent is still, today, just as it always has been, an improbable expedition that the road builders simply do not seem to be able to believe in at all. Only the rivers cut north and south through Kent and even then only four of the five main rivers flow northwards: the Darent, the Medway, and the Great and Little Stours. The fifth, the river Rother, follows the general pattern of the county's lineal features and flows eastward across Romney Marsh to the Channel.

Kent is divided, too, by the great variety of its countryside. The unusually long coastline varies from the creeks and salt flats of the north-west Kent Thames and Medway estuaries, to the world famous white chalk cliffs of Dover, and the unique shingle wilderness of Dungeness in the extreme south. There is the great protective arm of the Downs; the broad fertile lowlands of the Weald; and the up-tilted rim of the county that is still heavily wooded with the remains of the ancient High Wealden forest, teetering briefly above the Kent Ditch before plunging down again into the Sussex Weald beyond. In the north-west, industry crowds in upon the farms and market garden smallholdings; in the south-east, the Romney Marsh sheep are the undisputed lords of the levels. In north-east Kent, half the earliest history of England is impressed upon the few acres of Thanet: and in the south-west, the spin-off of the City's wealth into London's countryside has laid down more rich deposits of history in comparatively recent times. Finally, weaving among the physical and social divisions that rend the county are the the complementary and, at the same time, generally contradictory aims of developers and conservationists, progressives and traditionalists; each equally, but differently, anxious to contribute to the county's future.

The most subtle of the influences that divide the county, however, are those of the counter-magnets of London in the west and the Continent in the east. These two have been exerting their two-way pull on Kent for centuries, and bear some of the responsibilities for the tradition that distinguishes the Kentish Men from the Men of Kent. The historical characteristics that identify the two are, inevitably, fading now. But they were indentified particularly well by the late Richard Church in 1956 when he traced the Kentish Men in the west back to a blend of Saxon and Norman, "dour and unrelenting" but pleasant to live amongst. The Men of Kent, on the other hand, he defined as a "strange dark folk rather than a people," whose blood he suspected ran thinner and swifter than that of the Kentish Men, giving them a tendency to outbreaks of tragic-comedic mood that might end in a rebellion or a song. Except in a few of the more remote villages—and those mainly in East Kent now—those definitions would not, perhaps, bear very close inspection. The friendly reserve of the East Kent character lingers her and there, unalloyed by long intercourse with immigrants. In West Kent, the more militant independence bred from centuries of commerce with London is being more and more modified by the influx of people who do not, and whose children will not, think of themselves as Kentish Men.

When the Romans came to Kent, 2,000 years ago, they found the county inhabited by the Cantii. When they left, the Saxons founded here the Kingdom of the Cantings. Perhaps it will be in some such collective noun that the people of Kent will, before too long, have to resolve the ages-old dilemma that leaves no alternative to the 'ish' and the 'of' that distinguishes all that belongs in Kent.

Probably the last chance to perpetuate and formalize this division came when the report of the Redcliffe-Maud Commission on Local Government Reorganization in 1969 proposed that Kent should be divided into two administrative regions, one based on Maidstone, the other on Ashford. It was a proposal that found a good deal of support, particularly in East Kent, and if other issues had not moved the great British public to replace the Labour Government that set up the Redcliffe-Maud Commission, and so shelve the report, Kent might by now have joined Wessex and Mercia among the archives of administration. As it was, a Conservative Government alternative rushed through a reorganization scheme which, for all its imperfections, did at least leave the county undivided and confined within the boundaries it had shared with Sussex, Surrey and Greater London since 1965. That was when the London Government reorganization acknowledged the physical absorption of one-time Kent villages in the far-north-west, into the insatiable voracity of London, and scooped them up into the newly created London boroughs of Bromley and Bexley.

The villages of Kent, as of anywhere else, reflect pretty accurately the way in which the county developed during its long history of settlement.

The earliest inhabitants of Kent were hunting nomads who

roamed this way while the west coast of Britain was still the west coast of Europe. Caves near Ightham in West Kent were home to some of these early settlers, and they left some of their flint implements behind them when, for some unknown reason, they moved out.

Agriculture in Kent can be said to have begun with the arrival here during the New Stone (Neolithic) Age of a new wave of immigrants from the Mediterranean area, who cultivated small plots of land and kept cattle. These were the architects of the great stone structures of the Medway Valley that include Kit's Coty near Aylesford.

These first Kent farmers settled along the costal strip in the north, and spread inland along the river valleys. They probably lived in a sort of guarded peace with each other, sufficiently scattered to be able to avoid 'neighbours' while they wanted to, and this lasted until the coming of the first recognizably militant invaders in about 300 B.C. It was these invaders who made it necessary for the older settlers to build defensive hill forts all over the county, of which Oldbury, near Canterbury, was the largest. Canterbury was already, by this time, the largest and most important settlement in Kent.

The invading continentals were reinforced a century before the beginning of the Christian era by another group, remembered collectively as the Belgae, who came out of a Gaul that was by then part of the Roman Empire. The Belgae came first in raiding parties and later as an invasion force that conquered and then integrated with the natives. They took over Canterbury as their capital, and they brought with them new refinements in agricultural techniques, including a heavier plough than was previously know here. This made possible the cultivation of the less hospitable soils further inland from the sea and the rivers, and so continued the occupation of more and more of the Kentish countryside.

By this time there was a more or less established cross-Channel trade, and although tribal warfare was commonplace, Kent became noted as the most civilized part of Britain, comparatively densely populated and well-farmed, and so relatively prosperous.

This was the way the Romans found it when they made their first exploratory invasion in 55 and 54 B.C. It was still much the same a hundred years later when, in A.D. 43, the Emperor Claudius began his conquest of Britain with the historic landing at Rutupiae (which we now know as Richborough) at the southern end of the Wantsum Channel that then made Thanet a true island.

The conquest of east Kent was almost too easy for the disciplined legions, but the Kentish Men put up a good fight at the Medway crossing near Rochester before falling back on London in the face of the superior Roman skills at arms. After that, and for the next four hundred years, Kent was just a part—an important part —of the Roman province of Britain. Like other parts of the country, it benefited from the Roman order and engineering skills, and one of those roads, all of which led to Rome, linked London with Canterbury and the Channel Ports through Kent and became the fore-runner of today's A2 and the M2 motorway. Local iron ore was already being smelted in the Weald when the Romans arrived here, and one of the Roman roads ran from Rochester, through Maidstone, towards the south coast of Sussex.

The Roman era throughout southern Britain was generally one of peace and continuing prosperity. Apart from the main Roman towns of Canterbury, Dover and Rochester, there were a series of roadside camps and settlements, and a number of villas—outlying farmsteads and country houses—about sixty of which have been excavated in modern times.

But gradually, the attacks of the Northern European raiders on the British coastlines became more and more troublesome, and once the Romans had to withdraw from Britain in order to close the defences around the Roman home front, Britain and Kent were wide open for the raiders to abandon their hit and run tactics and to think in terms of invasion and colonization.

B

# Kent
# Villages

RNESS
MARGATE
Minster
Shurland
Warden Pt.
Eastchurch
Leysdown on Sea
HERNE BAY
Reculver
Birchington
St. Peters
Hillborough
Acol
Dumpton
Tankerton
Swalecliffe
St. Nicholas
WHITSTABLE
A299 Herne
Boyden at Wade
Manston
THE SWALE
Sarre
Minster
Harty Ferry
Heath
Chislet
Monkton
Ebbsfleet
RAMSGATE
Uplees
Seasalter
Grove
Conyer
Oare
Upstreet Ferry
W. Stourmouth
Graveney
Hersden
E. Stourmouth
Teynham
E. STOUR
Preston
Westmarsh
FAVERSHAM
Goodnestone
Broadoak
Westbere
Richborough
Ospringe
Preston
Blean
Sturry
Fordwich
Stodmarsh
Gt. Stonar
Hernhill
Wickhambreux
Newnham
Boughton
under Blean
Dunkirk
A2
CANTERBURY
Littlebourne
Wingham
Woodnesborough
Sheldwich
Chartham Hatch
A 2
Bramling
Ickham
Eastling
Bekesbourne
Staple
Worth
Throwley
Selling
Shottenden
Old Wives
Lees
Chartham
Patrixbourne
Goodnestone
Ham
Sholden
lisfield
Grn.
Shalmsford
St.
Neckington
Bridge
Chillenden
Betteshanger
DEAL
Leaveland
Chilham
Garlinge Grn.
Lt. Hardres
Adisham
Aylesham
Nonington
Northbourne
Godmersham
Petham
Bishopsbourne
Kingston
Womenswold
Tilmanstone
Barfreston
Solestreet
Barham
Eythorne
Sutton
Charing
Waltham
Upper
Hardres
Woolage
Green
Shepherdswell
W. Langdon
Westwell
Boughton Aluph
Stelling
Minnis
Wingmore
Coldred
E. Langdon
Kingsdown
Boughton Lees
Wye
Wootton
Guston
A20
Kennington
Hastingleigh
Elmsted
Court
Elham
Acrise
Lydden
Swingfield
St.
Temple Ewell
St. Margaret's
at Cliffe
Brook
Hinxhill
A2
SHFORD
Brabourne
Stowting
Densole
Swingfield
Minnis
Alkham
ersden
Willesborough
Lyminge
W. Hougham
Mersham
Smeeth
Etchinghill
Hawkinge
A20
DOVER
Sellindge
Paddlesworth
Capel le Ferne
E. STOUR
Postling
Newington
Clap Hill
Stanford
A20
Cheriton
D O V E R
rdchurch
Orlestone
Aldington
Saltwood
FOLKESTONE
Lumpne
rdington
Ruckinge
ROYAL MILITARY CANAL
Burmarsh
O F
Warehorne
Newchurch
Appledore
Snargate
St. Mary in
the Marsh
Dymchurch
Brenzett
St. Mary's Bay
Ivychurch
A259
Old Romney
Brookland
Littlestone on Sea
Walland Marsh
Greatstone on Sea
DUNGENESS

Legend rather than history tells us that King Vortigern of Kent invited two of the marauders, Hengist and Horsa, to join forces with him to keep out the rest and negotiated a land grant to secure their support. As a result, these two Jutish chieftains brought their followers to Kent and settled here, pushing the older inhabitants who were not enslaved or killed away to the west and south, or up into the hillier and less hospitable areas of the North Downs and the High Weald.

The Jutes were one group of the many from Northern Europe that we generally refer to now as the Saxons. They set up their own Kingdom in Kent which by A.D. 600 was chief of all the kingdoms south of the Humber. But two hundreds years later, Kent was part of Wessex, which in turn became the dominant Kingdom while Kent settled down to become just one of the shires of the Kingdom.

It was during the Saxon period that many of the villages of Kent settled down to become established centres of populations that were to last for 1,500 years. This was when Augustine made his historic landing at Ebbsfleet in Thanet with his forty monks from Rome and found a welcome from the Saxon King Ethelbert of Kent and his wife, who was already a Christian. By 597, Augustine was ready to be installed as the first Archbishop of Canterbury, head of the new Christian church in Britain. He instigated the long programme of church building that has been so useful to succeeding generations in establishing the antiquity of a great many villages.

Even at this time, though, there was very little communication between Kent and neighbouring Sussex to the south, beyond the then virtually impenetrable Andresweald (the High Wealden Forest). Although most of Kent—what might be called the Establishment—embraced Christianity so readily right at the beginning of the seventh century, Sussex was still almost wholly pagan for nearly another century.

There were pockets of paganism surviving in Kent, too, long after Augustine was dead. Many of the communities well removed

from the centres of Kentish (and British) Christianity at Canterbury and Rochester had virtually no contact with either. The
Thames Estuary and what was to become Romney Marsh were
both inhospitable swamps; the top of the North Downs offered
only land that was quite unattractive to the farming techniques of the day; and the High Weald was dense wood that
there was no reason to clear. There was a great deal of Kent left
for the still meagre population where the living was really quite
easy, and as the centuries passed, with very little to distinguish
one from another, the slowly growing population dotted these
areas with more and more settlements, many of which survived
to become the villages we cherish today.

The development of Kent was almost complete, as far as the
pattern of settlements goes, by the time of the Norman conquest,
with the first of the South Kent '-dens' and '-hursts' sufficiently
identifiable to earn mention in the Norman Domesday Survey and
to grow, in succeeding centuries, first as detached parts of the
north and west Kent manors, and later as centres of the
parishes as the concepts of local government developed.

One feature of Kent—unusual, but not quite unique to the
country—that shaped its later settlement pattern was the custom
of 'gavelkind'. This was the system of dividing inherited land
among all the sons of a land-owning family instead of, as in most
other parts of the country, an inheritance descending to the eldest
son.

Gavelkind meant that in Kent the land was fragmented (unless,
of course, a will specifically varied the custom, as it often did) and
this led to the creation of a large number of small holdings and
the familiar patchwork of hedge-stitched small fields. It is a
pattern that can baffle the amateur researcher and often creates
problems for the professionals when they have to sort out ownerships from the tangle of bequests and amalgamations and acquisitions and further bequests. It is a pattern, too, that is beginning
to change under the pressures of modern mechanized farming

methods, although there are some signs now that a reaction may be setting in as the disadvantages of wide open, hedgeless and often treeless acres are being weighed in the light of experience. The ravages of Dutch elm disease, which were particularly severe in many parts of North Kent, may provide landowners with opportunities to reverse a process that has been going on quite rapidly since the war by replacing the lost elms with new plantations of disease resistant trees that will restore the old leafiness to skylines that have become quite desolate and bleak.

Today, there are about one and a half million people living in Kent. Settlement tends to be characterized mainly by rail links with London, by which the new residents can commute to the capital. This has not been a wholly haphazard development, although it has reached a situation in which the county planners have to consider the capacity of the railways among the pros and cons of whether to allow new residential building.

The planners have had the advice of Professor Geoffrey Wibberley (among others) of Wye College. Wibberley, Professor of Countryside Planning of the University of London, has urged the protection from large scale residential development of all the North Kent agricultural areas, where the land is of exceptionally high quality, as well as Romney Marsh, the Medway Valley area, and other small areas of similarly high-quality farm land. He does not endear himself to the South Kent conservationists when he points out that there are areas of the Weald, the North Downs, and the Sevenoaks neighbourhood that could be spared for development much more easily. The difficulty is, of course, that these areas all tend to be of high amenity value, where sitting residents are prepared and, for the most part, particularly well able to put up a very vigorous fight against any such encroachment upon their stakes in the county. Nor is it difficult to sympathize with them. Practically the whole length of the North Downs, from the Medway to the Channel, is a designated area of outstanding natural beauty. Further west, the Downs are protected by inclusion in the

Metropolitan Green Belt which already reaches out to a roughly north-south line from the base of the Hoo Peninsula to the county boundary with Sussex below Tunbridge Wells, and will probably spread a bit more in the future, although at the expense of compensating losses of pockets surrendered to expansion of towns and villages inside the area.

As well as these heavily protected areas, the High Weald along the East Sussex boundary is designated as an area of great landscape value—one of a very exclusive few areas in the whole country to be so labelled. In all these areas development of all kinds is very carefully controlled in order not to spoil their essential characters.

North of the Downs, the exceptionally fertile fruit-growing region of North Kent reaches practically to the coast, and south of Maidstone the Mid-Kent fruit belt spreads out to the High Weald county boundary. The Thanet flatlands are already a heavy-yield vegetable growing region, and the Romney Marsh is a nationally important sheep-rearing area. Shade in those areas on the map of Kent and you see at a glance just how fine a line the planners have to draw between the demands of environment and agriculture, and the clamorous and no less real needs of home-seekers and the industrialists who can provide employment for them.

Add to the broad sweeps of protected countryside nearly three hundred more or less small areas which have already been identified as potential conservation areas, where it is the intention to preserve the character of the area without necessarily identifying any one feature of the area as specially worthy of protection, and the problem becomes a little more complex. Many of these conservation areas are in villages, and although they do not put any blanket clamp-down on new buildings, they do try to ensure that any new building that does take place inside the conservation area is of a high quality and blends with the existing surroundings. It is a limiting factor in considering planning applications from would-be developers.

Finally, there are more than 155 scheduled ancient monuments in Kent and more than 5,000 buildings listed as of special architectural or historic interest, with another 7,000-plus on the government's supplementary list.

But town and country planning is still a comparatively new science. Its practitioners are still learning, not only how to use the skills they have acquired, but also what new skills are needed to tackle new problems that are revealed to them all the time.

There is certainly no unanimity about what planners ought to be aiming at—except possibly that it is generally agreed that they very seldom actually do the right thing! They tread a difficult path between the needs of some and the wishes of others, so that they are always either protectors or ravagers—and usually both at the same time. I am not a planner, so I know exactly how to deal with most of the planning problems that present themselves to public scrutiny from time to time. But even I am not sure quite how the planners should be coaxing some of our villages into the twenty-first century that is just ahead.

The problem is by no means exclusive to Kent, of course, but Kent is one of the counties where it is specially acute. Are we right, for instance, to try to preserve what we call the essential character of our villages? For that matter, are we sure we are all talking about the same thing when we discuss what is the essential character of a village? Perhaps we should be asking ourselves if the day of the village as a community concept is past, or passing, though not necessarily for ever. Certainly, very few of the villages are dependent upon the local agriculture as they were even as recently, as say, fifty years ago.

Farming has joined the mechanized industries, and quite large farming units today can be operated very efficiently with far fewer employees than they once needed. So the villagers, particularly the young ones, when they leave school, look away from the village for work. Greater individual mobility has made it perfectly realistic for them to seek fulfilment of their ambitions in towns that may be quite long distances from home. And when they find it, they do not usually look back to the village of their birth for their own family home, when that time comes. As they move away, their places in the villages are being taken by successful town dwellers in search of havens from the pressures of their own achievements: second-home seekers who want a holiday or week-end retreat from London and other big towns and cities, to which they can eventually retire. For them, a country property is an investment, a way of safeguarding capital against the effects of inflation and a comforting buffer against old age. They are prepared to pay well for the qualities they prize: picturesque surroundings, peace, quiet and a measure of seclusion that does not trespass too far upon accessibility. If the property they choose needs to be restored, or if a group of cottages must be converted into one in order to make it large enough to offer the sort of spaciousness the new owners regard as necessary, they can afford to do the necessary work. When it is done, the remodelled property's market value has been very much enhanced, as well as its suitability as a modern home.

A recent survey revealed that Kent has a very large proportion of 'second home' residents, but it is difficult to criticize the trend too harshly. It can, after all, be credited with helping to preserve some of the most visually attractive features of the county. The alternative would often be demolition and redevelopment which would contribute little towards meeting the need for homes, since the people who most need cheap housing do not, generally, want to live in the villages, and those who want to become the new villagers are not looking for cheap housing.

Nevertheless, the 'second home' syndrome in the villages is changing their character, creating enclaves of mainly middle-aged and elderly, middle and upper-class 'immigrants' who often lack the strong sense of community that once characterized village life. Indeed, often the newcomers do not integrate with the natives at all; they do not share the same ambitions for the village, and they are, at the same time, often far better equipped with expertise, time and money to contest any planned alterations to their chosen environment.

Present plans are not to bloat existing villages but to control their development and to house and employ the natural population increase in a series of newly-created towns. The county development plan assumes that the most densely populated areas of Kent by 1981 will be the Medway Towns (Chatham, Rochester, Strood and Gillingham), Thames-side (around Dartford and Gravesend), the Isle of Thanet, and Maidstone, with the Channel Ports, Tunbridge Wells and Ashford following on. The two areas of fastest growth will be the Isle of Sheppey and Ashford, and there has been talk, too, of encouraging the growth of the mining village of Aylesham, west of Dover, until it is a quite large town. All this will have a considerable impact on the rural areas between existing villages if not, directly, on the villages themselves.

One way and another, there is no doubt that the face of rural Kent is due to change radically in the next decade or so. Forecasts generally agree that the county is going to have to cope with a new popularity as a place to live, a place to visit, and a place to pass through. The very proximity to the European mainland promises, with or without a Channel tunnel, to increase enormously the volume of traffic on Kent roads, as well as the pressures for development of storage, warehousing and other service industries.

Argument rages perhaps particularly strongly in Kent, where it is, after all, no mere academic topic, but a very closely consequential matter, about whether the tunnel would soften the impact of the traffic or make it worse. Opponents fear the tunnel would serve to funnel into Kent even more traffic, streaming from all directions towards the common goal of the Cheriton terminal. Supporters hope that the effect would be to siphon traffic out of the villages and the countryside, and concentrate it into the main rail and road approach routes, where it would, at any rate, be contained in a comparatively narrow corridor. The future has been clouded by the dawning realization that we are living on borrowed oil anyway, and that the increase in road traffic may have been very much over-estimated hitherto. The new situation has yet to be appraised properly, but it is likely to make the tunnel more rather than less necessary. There may be a shift of emphasis within the arguments about the effect of the tunnel on the county at large; it will not end the arguments themselves.

All good Englishmen, naturally, find it impossible to be wholly happy about their new European status. But if we had to abandon the historical British "sceptred isle" role, it seems to be reasonable, now, to draw as close as possible to our new in-laws. And since we cannot do anything about physically coming alongside the European mainland, the tunnel is probably the next best thing. Its direct effect on Kent villages may well be minimal. Its indirect effect, though, may well not be. Kent is still the garden of England, and the garden path is used by the nation's tradesmen as well as by its guests. Kent cannot simply turn its back proudly on the people who want to come through the garden gate as though it thought they had no business on such hallowed soil. It may be that the only practical role for the villages in the foreseeable future will be that of 'leisure satellites' rather than the sort of self-sustaining centres of industry—whether that industry is agriculture or something else—that they once were. The important thing, though, is that they should remain alive, and make a positive contribution to the life of the county, as they have done for two thousand years.

In whatever role they are cast in the future, the danger surely is that they will be over-protected; molly-coddled to the point where they withdraw from the twentieth century altogether, as though it were something that did not concern them. The twentieth century, no less than any of the others that have handed the villages down to us as they are today, must contribute something of itself to the villages so that we, in our turn, can hand them on to be admired, enjoyed and (most of all) used by those who come after us.

Of course we are proud of our villages. Of course we should cherish and defend them. But it would be a pity if, in fear of spoiling them, we timidly allowed them to become mere time-passed exhibits.

# 2

# North Kent

THE North Kent coastline is esturial, even at the eastern tip, where Thanet sticks its nose up at the receding French coast, across the Channel. It is a long, thin strip of mainly marshlands, creased by creeks and inlets, wild and, where it has been drained, fertile. It reaches out from the feet of the North Downs to the sea all the way from the Greater London boundary east of Dartford along to the Isle of Thanet. Although the whole length irrefutably faces north, natives of Kent will not think it at all strange if North Kent is separated from North-East Kent and Thanet at the Faversham and Graveney Marshes. To me, it is wholly natural to think of the coast west of this area as North Kent and if visitors to the county find this division at all odd let them ask themselves if their own counties do not have similar peculiarities.

The Graveney marshes provide an introduction to the character of the whole coastal strip: flat pastures for the most part, patched with cereals and root crops, creased with creeks and small waterways and lined with drainage ditches. The ravages of Dutch elm disease have scarred the region particularly sadly with bare, dead trees that somehow look wholly natural in their bleak surroundings. There is a distinctive wild fascination about the whole coastline that is not unlike that of Romney Marsh in some ways—although no-one would ever confuse the two. Much of the foreshore and the wilder acres of backing marshlands are protected as areas of special scientific interest because of the rarity of the plant and animal wildlife. Botanists and birdwatchers alike have been known to become ecstatic—in their undemonstrative scientific way, naturally—as they bend into the winds that always seem to blow across these lowlying flat lands and search out new and unique habitats. Wholly unscientific artists find the landscaping and the native wildlife a source of endless inspiration, and even simple stand-and-stare wastrels like myself, arrived with no motive other than to soak up the special atmosphere of the places, find a soul-soothing solitude that is quite as rare as anything that lives there.

In 1971 a Nature Conservancy working party produced a very detailed report about this whole North Kent coastline, from Cliffe in the west to Seasalter, pointing out that this area has long been recognized as of outstanding national and even international scientific importance. Among other authorities who have recognized the value of the coastline were the authors of the Government's strategic plan for the South-East which, in 1970, named the North Kent marshes as an area of significant environmental resources.

One of many unique features of the area is the way the remoteness of the marshes and the very gradual slope of the land into the sea which creates miles of low-water mudflats has provided one of the most important havens for migrating birds in all North-West Europe. Since the Nature Conservancy report was published, part of the coastline east of Faversham Creek has been designated a protected area, and this should go some way to ensuring that the quality of the area is preserved in the face of ever increasing demands for water sport activities.

But, in general, here as elsewhere, man and the rest of nature live only grudgingly side by side. Most of the coast is hemmed with new sea walls which make it possible to farm the land behind them much more intensively than it once was. That is splendid for the land owners, of course, but very much less inviting for the birds, which preferred things the way they used to be.

On the Isle of Grain, in the Thames estuary, a big oil refinery has brought many changes, and the power station at Hoo has added its contribution to the changes. The marshes are valued and championed, but the challengers keep them under attack and when they win a round it tends to be by a bigger margin than when the defenders score.

There is a fine introductory view of the Graveney marshes, the Swale (never, please the river Swale—but I must admit I have never met anyone who could satisfactorily explain why not!) and the hump of the Isle of Sheppey pushing up into the Thames and Medway estuary to be seen from the top of Boughton Hill, the highest point of the A2 road between Faversham and Canterbury. The hill drops away steeply into the stretched-out village of Boughton, one of a series of sorely-tested A2 villages soon, hopefully, to be bypassed and relieved of the heavy traffic that has made the village main street—always a well-travelled highway—into a noisy, dirty, dangerous canyon of misery for the residents. When the traffic thunders past instead of through the village, we can all enjoy again the wide variety of architectural styles along both sides of the road, from the modern, estate-style homes that greet arrivals from the east, to the medieval timbered and Georgian stuccoed homes that watch them leave again at the western end.

A mile west of Boughton, at Brenley Corner, the M2 emerges from its underpass to join the Thanet Way and thereafter North Kent is separated into three strips: that between the sea and the A2; the area between the A2 and the roughly parallel M2; and the southern slopes of the North Downs themselves.

The first of these strips are the marshlands, which are very sparsely populated indeed, although in the past twenty years or so the growth of caravan and chalet villages has gone some way towards changing this. Seasalter, for instance, is almost all chalets and caravans. Immediately west of Whitstable, it was once a desolate haunt of smugglers and, as the name suggests, of people (mostly shell-fishers) who also harvested the sea's salt. Saltings were once a common feature of the whole coastline: broad flat areas behind the high tide mark, where the sea could be coaxed to flood into areas surrounded by low earth walls. When the tide went out, the water remaining was evaporated and the deposited salt gathered and marketed.

The last time the sea renewed its ages old acquaintance with the Seasalter saltings on any appreciable scale was in 1963. Then, acres of the land behind the old sea wall (the wall has been re-built since then) lay under water for weeks, and the land was poisoned by the quantities of salt that soaked into it. It was years before it was fit for normal farming again.

There is still an air of desolation about the whole area in the winter. In the summer, though, Seasalter rivals the Thanet resorts of Ramsgate and Margate with holidaymakers and the roadside verges become one continuous car park below the 'promenade' created by the top of the new, higher sea wall.

The Thanet–London railway crosses Seasalter Level, the net-work of drainage ditches create a landscape of grazing pasture very reminiscent of East Anglia, and one ditch, in 1971, yielded up a 2,000 year-old secret during dredging operations when the remains of a Viking ship were found in the mud. The ship was something of a nine days' wonder to local people and visitors who trekked across the spongy turf from the Seasalter–Faversham road, only to find the old timbers completely hidden from view beneath the archae-ologists' protective tarpaulins. Even those few visitors who did see the skeletal timbers fleshy with marsh mud were apt to wonder what all the fuss was about; but the experts who came to look at the find practically danced a hornpipe in their excitement. It was, in fact, the best-preserved Viking vessel ever found in England and it is now lodged at Greenwich Maritime Museum, a perpetual reference to the preservative qualities of the Seasalter marsh mud.

The railway goes under a bridge at Graveney village, which would be no more than a hamlet of cottages grouped near the farms hereabouts if it were not for the unattractive group of council houses, mainly near the little school, that have boosted the

The original of Joe Gargery's forge at High Halstow

The Old Keep, Cooling Castle

Charles Dickens' last house, Gad's Hill Place, now a girls' school


An old village tradition: cricket on the green, Meopham

Not all villages are picturesque—a caravan 'village' at Seasalter


A wholly twentieth-century village—Vigo new village

A Christmas card scene: 'The Leather Bottle' at Cobham

local population since the war. The rather fine fourteenth century church stands a little aloof from the village, but it has a rather specially notable oak roof, a carved Tudor screen and a pulpit that is said to have been carved by the Master, Grinling Gibbons himself.

From Graveney, a belt of orchards slightly higher than the marshes themselves, reaches out towards Faversham Creek, which snakes in from the Swale and is the main reason why the town and port of Faversham is where it is. The land here, and stretching in a belt all the way to the Medway Towns is some of the highest quality agricultural land in the country. This was the land that helped earn for Kent the title of 'Garden of England' with its orchards, a few hop gardens, cereals, root crops, strawberries and other top fruits—there are parts of this whole region where a fresh cut pole planted as a wash-line post will sprout leaves and take root just for the sheer joy of living in such soil!

Goodnestone is a near neighbour of Graveney, but a true hamlet along the road towards Faversham, mainly identified from the road by the local police house and by a rather massive-looking roadside oast house group which has recently been converted into semi-detached but very distinctive private homes, with square kilns at each end.

The town of Faversham is itself a little gem that hangs pendant-like from the ribbon of the A2 and although it is certainly no village, a mention in passing is surely in order, especially as Davington village, next along the North Kent coastal strip, is really part of the town. Part, that is, in that the old borough boundary was flung round it in 1935. But in spite of the very considerable amount of new council house building on this side of the town, Davington has clung to its village characteristics, dominated entirely by the Priory and the mellow red brick building that was once the Davington Farm house.

The land rises abruptly up out of Faversham Creek into Davington, the twelfth-century Priory and church and the old Davington

Court which was from very early times the home of the Earls of Athol. It was demolished some years ago and replaced by old people's homes, but the old gateway to the house has been preserved, to stare blindly out into (inevitably, perhaps) Old Gate Road which is part of the new private estates.

The Priory is still there, though, a grey stone memorial to its founder, Fulk de Newenham, who built it in 1153 for Benedictine nuns who lived in seclusion there for four hundred years. Then came a period of dispute with the monks of Faversham Abbey and by 1527 there was only the Prioress, one nun and a lay sister living in the Priory. After the Prioress died in March 1534, the Priory became derelict until it was taken over by Henry VIII, who gave it to Sir Thomas Cheney.

Beyond Davington, the road meanders on past gravel workings —some of which provide very good angling; others provide Faversham ratepayers with a tip for their refuse—and a little industrial estate on the edge of which stands a distinctive old windmill which has been saved from dereliction, restored and converted into a very comfortable private home.

This is the Oare windmill, not to be confused with 'The Windmill' at Oare (which is a public house a little way further along the same road). Oare Creek pushes a muddy little finger almost to the road at this point, an offshoot of the larger Faversham Creek and a well-known haven for small craft, pleasure-bent in the waters of the estuary, and also for a few resident houseboats.

Just as Davington Hill rises steeply up from Faversham Creek, so the village of Oare seems to scramble up out of reach of any threats of flooding from Oare Creek. The village is almost wholly on top of the hill; a small, rather charming but not specially distinguished group of mainly redbrick terrace houses, from which one road slews off towards Harty Ferry, where at low tide a causeway dips down into the water west of Horse Sands, and emerges at the Ferry Inn on the Isle of Sheppey, across the Swale.

Alternatively, the road from Oare will take the traveller to the dead end that is the marshlands hamlet of Uplees, or through the steeply sloping woodlands above Luddenham marshes, past ancient Luddenham Court, now a farmhouse, and back on to the A2 at the bottom of Beacon Hill. This is one of many hills behind the coastline that earned its name in the days when hilltop beacons were both an aid to navigation and a warning of danger of attack from the sea.

Teynham sprawls alongside the A2 which is its main street, doing its best to look attractive with its weather-boarding and old tiling, but not really succeeding. At the west end of the A2, the village peters out into the surrounding orchards, as do the newer parts of the village between the road and the railway. Teynham is the birthplace of the Kentish cherry and apple orchards. It was here that Henry VIII's fruiterer, Richard Harris, planted his continental cherries and apple trees. Today, the village is still a centre of the North Kent fruit belt and the house owned by Richard Harris, at Newgardens, Conyer, still stands.

Conyer is scarcely large enough to deserve the title of village, yet it is a bustling place throughout the summer, when the creekside marina is thronged with pipe-smoking men in blue jersey and plimsolls all intent on getting the last dregs of off-duty pleasure out of messing about in their boats.

The agricultural village of Tonge had a mill in the days when the Domesday Survey noted such features, and today there is still a Tonge Mill, very probably on the same site, between the road through the village and the railway. The present mill, though, is eighteenth century, and was saved in 1971 by £2,000 worth of repairs to the roof from joining its fore-runners. It stands alongside all that remains of Tonge Castle, now no more than a dry moat round an 80 foot high grassy mound, but once an impressive motte and bailey Norman castle on the site of an earlier earthen stronghold built by the Jutish chieftain Hengist.

It was at Tonge that the King of Kent, Vortigern, met the invading Hengist and offered him as much land as he could cover with a single ox hide. The wily Jute accepted the offer, had a hide cut into thongs which he laid end to end round an area of land equivalent to many 'hides', and so created a new land measure and gave the village its name as well.

Out on the marshes flanking Milton Creek, Murston is another of those communities that almost seem to have turned their backs on the world and decided to sulk until an out-of-sympathy world relents and acknowledges their qualities. There is a distinctive character about these marsh villages and it is easy to understand why the Churches Committee of the Kent Archaeological Society should be so anxious to preserve Murston's fourteenth-century church against the demolition designs of the Diocesan Council. There are no plans at present for devolpment of the land around the church, but it is an area of high pressures for housing and if there were any building there the restored church could be a most attractive centre piece for it, as well as rediscovering a place for itself in the local community.

Another of the Watling Street (A2) villages is Bapchild, a few shops and houses alongside the road dwindling away into scattered cottages and farm buildings on either side. To motorists on the road, the need to negotiate the parked cars and vans is about all that draws attention to the village at all, yet it was at Bapchild, in the eighth century, that two kings of Kent held important councils and a spring on the village outskirts, still known locally as Becket's Well, marks the spot where a pilgrims' oratory once stood. So, whatever the status of Bapchild today, it has had its moments in the past.

After Bapchild the road, disdainful of our present preoccupation with villages, surges through the wholly unattractive main street area of the town of Sittingbourne and Milton Regis, to reach the Key Street crossroads.

Straight ahead lies Rainham and Gillingham and the conurbation that is the Medway Towns. To the left, Maidstone. But the road to the right is the only highway there is to the Isle of Sheppey. Frankly, it is not much of a highway, as highways go. There are plans to improve it, and if the plans that also exist to encourage a very considerable development of the island, including the possible provision of homes for overspilling Londoners, then the road improvement may come more quickly than is otherwise likely.

But, so far, we are lucky; the road is good enough for comfort, through Bobbing where Titus Oates was once vicar, past Bobbing Court, and on to Iwade, where the faithful are called to worship in the little old church by bells almost as old as the fourteenth-century bell tower itself.

On the way to Iwade, the road by-passes Kemsley and the Bowater Corporation paper mill alongside Milton Creek which, in fact, reaches into Sittingbourne and is the home of the Thames and Medway Barge Museum which is well worth a visit to look at the paintings and photographs and models of some of the famous old barges that once plied the North Kent creeks and coastline.

Kemsley paper mill is certainly no beauty and the village which was built between the wars for the mill workers is not particularly beautiful, either. But it does have what must be the most exclusive passenger railway station in Kent. For the only way to reach Kemsley Down station is by train: there is no other public right of way to it. It is at the end of a two-mile single-track railway line that links the Kemsley mill with Sittingbourne mill, the Sittingbourne and Kemsley Light Railway (S.K.L.R.) and throughout the summer, a small subscription to the Locomotive Club of Great Britain buys for hundreds of enthusiasts as many rides as they have stamina for on the only preserved narrow gauge industrial railway in South-East England.

Iwade—which was where we were bound for before the S.K.L.R. diverted us—is a marsh village, the last outpost of mainland community life before the road straightens itself to take the shortest distance possible across the featureless base of the Chetney peninsula in order to reach and cross the Kingsferry Bridge to the Minster Marshes on the Isle of Sheppey.

Sheppey rises very gently out of the Swale, which is quite narrow at this point and about two-thirds of the southern side of the island is almost completely flat, crinkled with creeks and inlets and networks of ditches linking larger waterways. In the centre, on rising ground just behind Eastchurch Marshes, is H. M. Prison, visible, but pushed out, from the village of Eastchurch on the end of a road that, symbolically, leads nowhere else. All the heavy concentration of homes and industry is the north-west corner of the island, where ancient Queenborough and the sprawling residential areas of Halfway Houses and Minster form a reef behind which dockland Sheerness is steadily growing into Kent's number two port, second only to Dover. For the rest, the island offers its visitors any amount of easy walking, pleasant beaches, some cliff-top views at, for example, Warden Point on the north-east corner, and holiday camps—a large number of holiday camps.

Eastchurch is a pretty, wooded village astride the Island's only east-west main road. It is fairly quiet nowadays, but the village was well-known to aviation pioneers. Lord Brabazon of Tara (whose niche in history will for ever be decorated with his Pilot's Licence No. 1) and Sir Winston Churchill both learned to fly at Eastchurch aerodrome, and two other earlier flyers, C. S. Rolls and Cecil Grace, both died tragically at Eastchurch. Nearby the ruins of the sixteenth-century Shurland Hall recall the ill-fated honeymooners, Henry VIII and Anne Boleyn, who stayed there.

Quite different in character is Leysdown, with its sea wall promenade and its wide, sloping beaches, which looks back perhaps just a little wistfully, upon its village days before the twenty-two different holiday camps bloated it to undeniable town size and life-style.

But not far away is Warden, which remains attractively picturesque on the side of the sharp slope up from Leysdown to the Warden Point cliff tops. Once a stronghold of pirates and smugglers, it took its name from the king's officer who was installed here specifically to discourage such lawlessness. Local legend insists that there is a tunnel which links Warden Manor with the old Shurland Castle, now in ruins outside Eastchurch. But no-one has ever been able to find it.

The village Post Office at Warden was once the 'Smack Aground' inn, and home of a notorious smuggler who was finally deported to Australia in the eighteenth century. The sea which gave Warden its living in those days, has claimed its own since then, and most of the  hundred cottages that were the old village, together with its church, have fallen into the sea, which has eaten away the cliff.

As places like Leysdown have outgrown their village status, others, like Elmley, have shrunk. Elmley is no longer a village, but once it had a cement works which employed a fairly large local resident workforce. The works have been closed for many years now, and the workers have all drifted elsewhere. Today, Elmley Marshes are as desolate and lovely in their own peculiar way as anywhere in all Kent. Just to stand there on a grey, windy day at the wildfowlers' end of the year is to understand how it is that some authorities declare the name Elmley derives from the name for a place of sacrifice where Druids once presided over long forgotten rites and festivals.

In the south of Sheppey, Harty is little more than the Ferry Inn on the marshes that are technically the separate Isle of Harty because of the way the Capel Fleet wriggles through from Eastchurch to Leysdown marshes. The Inn is worth a visit, though: an old timbered building, made welcoming to modern visitors with a wide terrace jutting out into the grass slope down to the Swale. The Ferry Inn offers a pleasant enough resting spot where Sheppey visitors can restore the tissues a bit before retracing their path back to the main road and returning—of necessity along the same outward route, since it is the only one—to the mainland.

The diversion to Sheppey began at Key Street, on the A2. If it had not, the alternative was to go on through the very heart of the cherry orchard country around Sittingbourne to Newington, a part of the Watling Street area very familiar to the Romans, who left their characteristic litter everywhere.

Thomas à Becket is said to have stayed at Newington on his way to Canterbury for the last time, and near the church are two sarsen stones of very ancient origin but uncertain purpose. One of the two is known as the Devil's Stone. There is, of course, a local legend to account for this: that the devil was so angered by the clamour of the church bells that he stole them one night. But in jumping down from the tower with them, he fell over the stone, and the bells rolled into a stream which, thereafter, for ever ran "clear as a bell".

A road from Newington starts a loop that links Lower Halstow, on the creek-cracked Medway estuary, with Upchurch, where the local gravel pits have yielded up prehistoric evidence of centuries of habitation. A great deal of Roman pottery has come to light at Upchurch, too—not surprisingly, for it was here that the Romans had one of the most important of their early English potteries.

Much more recently, Upchurch was distinguished by having for its vicar for six years, from 1560 to 1566, the father of Sir Francis Drake, and he is buried in the churchyard there, in the shadow of the unusually part square, part octagonal church tower topped by a shingled spire which was and is still a navigational landmark for vessels in the Medway estuary.

Back to the A2 again, and almost the whole of the next eight or nine miles passes through the wholly built-up urban areas of Rainham, Gillingham, Chatham, Rochester and Strood, beyond which it is possible to turn northwards again and search out the fascination of the Hoo Peninsula marshes.

The peninsula slopes up out of the estuary into a ridge of higher land that forms its backbone and throws back good farming land on either side into the marshes, oozes, flats and saltings of the Thames on the west and the Medway on the east. It is a wild, desolate place for the most part, probably very little different today from when smugglers used its creeks two and three centuries ago. Then, however, there was no need to protect the interests of the teeming wildlife—they were not threatened. Today there is, and every proposal to bring development to the peninsula is assured in advance of an outcry against a new threat to the unique wildlife interest of the whole area. The threats are constant, and it is difficult to see how, particularly if the Maplin development on the Essex coast goes ahead as it seems certain to do, the strong arguments in favour of filling in this whole area with the industry and the associated residential areas that are predicted for Kent in the next twenty years, will be rebutted.

Immediately beyond Rochester, and by no means easy to distinguish from the city is Frindsbury, much of which is, in any case, within the city's boundaries now. Neighbouring Wainscott clings pretty precariously to what remains of its village identity on the very edge of the Rochester–Strood–Frindsbury urban area, too. But Upnor, by contrast, is almost remote still; a village with that easy-going, relaxed air that always seems to belong with river-side dwellers. Its water front curves round the river Medway's last convulsive twitch before it straightens and widens and gets ready to slough its banks and revel in the welcome of the estuary.

Today, Upnor is one of the Medway's major yachting and water sports centres. Anchored here is the training ship *Arethusa*, once the four-masted barque *Peking* before it became the floating school administered by the Shaftesbury Homes Society. Now its future is in doubt since the owners announced it would cost £100,000 to renovate the vessel.

Just behind the Upnor foreshore are the ragstone remains of Upnor Castle, built on the orders of Elizabeth I in 1561 to defend Chatham dockyards on the opposite bank. It was not until more than a century later that the castle was called into action when, on 10th June 1667, the Dutch fleet sailed into the Medway. The Upnor garrison came under fire, but gave as good as they got and sank several of the Dutch ships, so that the impudent Netherlanders were dissuaded from any ideas they had about penetrating further inland.

The village is nominally separated into Upper and Lower Upnor and immediately inland from Lower Upnor the land rises to the crest of Beacon Hill and Chattenden, most of which is barracks, almost exactly midway between Wainscott and Hoo.

The whole of this peninsula takes its name from the village of Hoo St Werburgh which, in turn, took its name from the daughter of the seventh-century King of Mercia, Wulfhere. St Werburgh founded a nunnery at Hoo. It was destroyed by Viking raiders and the founder's body was removed to Chester, where it remained. The church of St Werburgh is worth a visit for its particularly fine collection of memorial brasses, and because it is generally accepted as the church with the finest tower and the tallest spire in the neighbourhood.

The village stands amid rich farming and marsh pasture land, although there has been a good deal of development of this part of the peninsula in recent years, including the 2,000 megawatt Kingsnorth electricity generating station, which has led to a boom in house building for the workers there, and for others who work on the nearby Isle of Grain.

One of the few remaining heronries in Kent and one of the largest in the country is to be found near the village of High Halstow which looks out over the neighbouring marshes from a little eminence. No-one really knows for sure when the work of reclaiming these marshes began. Probably the Romans had a hand in it, but certainly most of it was done by Dutch workmen and engineers in the seventeenth century. The result has been to provide Kent with many acres of fine pasture land that would otherwise have been salt-soured waste.

All the way out from High Halstow to the estuary coastline there are occasional isolated farms and buildings, but none more isolated than Shade House on Halstow Marshes, and none more credibly associated with the good old days when smuggling was thought of not so much as law-breaking but as a righteous assertion of free trading rights no Government could properly interfere with.

All of this, of course, is part of Dickens country, and there is a half-timbered cottage in High Halstow which was once the local forge, and which is said to have been the model for Joe Gargery's forge in Dickens' novel, *Great Expectations*.

Now, let's get this next one right: St Mary's Hoo is the name of the village. It is the parish that drops the possessive and becomes St Mary Hoo. There may even be a good reason for that, though I do not know what it is.

It is a pleasant little village, the first we have come to on the peninsula that looks like a village should: a few cottages, farmhouses, the church and the old rectory, and a duckpond. All just high enough above sea level to give a first-class view out over the miles of fertile marshlands on all sides. Once upon a time, it was a favoured spot for the wealthy to retreat to, and there were several manor houses hereabouts. They have long since gone, and today few people visit the village at all. But in the mid-nineteenth century, the village enjoyed a certain prosperity as a result of the farming methods introduced in the locality by Mr Henry Pye—known locally as the King of the Hundred of Hoo. He came to farm at St Mary's Hall in 1845, carried out extensive drainage schemes, and introduced mechanization to local farming with steam ploughing and threshing and seed cultivation.

Before that, the village attracted some little notoriety from having the Reverend Robert Burt as its rector—bought by him with the hush-money he received for marrying secretly (and illegally) Maria Fitzherbert and the future King George IV. The vicar's secret did not come to light until 114 years after the ceremony, and in that time his son, the Reverend Robert Gascoyne Burt, had added to the family legends such personal eccentricities as segregating men, women and children in different parts of the church, and employing the village band to provide music for the church services. Still, he had his good points, too; one of them was that he never, in all the fifty-nine years he was at High Halstow, preached a sermon.

Allhallows—properly Hoo Allhallows—is a very small village today, but it almost passed out of existence altogether in the eighteenth and nineteenth centuries after being a flourishing little community in the sixteenth century. It was a railway that revived it. A station was built at nearby Allhallows-on-Sea in 1932, the river frontage there was developed into a popular resort, and so it has remained to the present time. The railway is closed now and, in spite of local attempts to reopen it, looks like remaining closed. But the road is reasonably good, and the area is now one of caravan sites and chalets. One local authority caravan estate alone has six hundred caravans on it and the population is a shifting holidaymaking one of several thousands every year.

Between the old village and the resort and, indeed, on either side, the flat lands are a wildfowler's paradise. They extend across to the Isle of Grain, which is separated from the rest of the peninsula by Yantlet Creek, at the mouth of which is a stone obelisk marking the limit of the Port of London Authority's control over the river. The creek silted up during the eighteenth century, and in 1823 a ditch was cut to allow boats to pass between Grain and the mainland again. But people on both sides of the waterway protested and appealed to the Crown so that after eighteen months a Special Jury of Surrey Assizes ruled that the Corporation of the City of London had gone too far in having the creek made navigable again. They ordered that the causeway and the road linking the two sides should be restored.

In 1882, Port Victoria was built around the railhead and pier on the Isle of Grain, but although Queen Victoria used it to embark upon cross-Channel voyages, it never achieved the hoped-for popularity and during the First World War the pier station was dismantled.

In 1923, though, Grain received another boost when the first oil refinery was built just south-west of the village. Thirty years later, the huge BP Kent Oil Refinery came into use and now about half the total acreage of the Isle of Grain is taken up by the tangle of refinery equipment and storage tanks, and the tall chimneys are visible from the North Downs above Maidstone, ten or twelve miles away. Now, the refinery has a new neighbour in the Isle of Grain power station, and other heavy industrial interests cast eyes on what remains of the island's acreage from time to time.

Back on the mainland, Stoke and Lower Stoke are two separated settlements. Stoke has brooded over the low-water mudbanks and the islets and coves of the Medway's north bank for more than 1,000 years, and got itself written into history for the first time in a document of 738, long before it was described in the Domesday survey.

Like so much of this part of Kent, Stoke has been under flood water many times during its history. The last serious flooding was in1968, and that would have seemed more serious if the villagers did not still remember so very vividly the Great Flood of 1953 when the Yantlet Channel became two miles of floodwater and no-one ever did put a final figure to the cost to Kent.

One of the marsh outposts is Cooling, less distinguished as a village than as the site of Cooling Castle, and for the thirteen small gravestones in the churchyard of St James' Church, identified with the graves of Pip's brothers as described by Charles Dickens in his book *Great Expectations*.

The castle is privately owned and little more than the keep remains of the original building. But it is still occupied and the keep towers stand as a memorial to an interesting if violent history stretching back to the ninth-century manor house home of Alduf, servant of King Coenulf of Mercia. Built after a French sea raid in 1379, when Sir John de Cobham got permission to fortify his new manor house at Cooling, the castle was, at one period, the home of that Sir John Oldcastle who may have been Shakespeare's model for his Falstaff. In 1554 it was captured by Sir Thomas Wyatt and his rebels after a gun battle that left cannon balls in the moat to be discovered four hundred years later. The present house dates from about 1670 and is not normally open to the public.

Although a reasonably-sized village today, Cliffe-at-Hoo was much bigger 450 years ago. It was, in fact, quite a sizeable town when it was destroyed by fire in 1520 and had enjoyed a position of some importance since Saxon times.

During the eighth and ninth centuries, Saxon church leaders gathered at Cliffe for their national synods, usually headed by the Kings of Mercia and the Archbishops of Canterbury. Even today, the parish church of St Helen (a descendent of an original church founded by King Offa of Mercia in 774) is one of the best in Kent and, incidentally, the only one in the county with that particular dedication. It has a 100 foot nave, medieval wall paintings, and one of the finest silver-gilt pre-Reformation patens (1525) to be seen anywhere.

It was the Victorian building boom and the arrival of cement works to the Medway's banks that began Cliffe's return to prosperity, bolstered more recently still by the local petrol storage depot.

Higham invokes memories of Dickens again, for just outside the village is Gad's Hill, once notorious for highwaymen who for two hundred years, throughout most of the seventeenth and eighteenth centuries, made it one of the most dreaded stretches of road in all England.

That reputation, though, was history by the time Charles Dickens bought Gad's Hill Place in 1856, where he was to spend his last fifteen years in fulfilment of a boyish ambition. Quite what it was about this rather undistinguished brick house with the white cupola on top that so appealed to the young Dickens is difficult to see. If he had seen it today, we might have wondered if its use as a girls' school had something to do with it!

The A226 road links Rochester and Strood with Gravesend across the bottom of the Hoo Peninsula and, after it goes through the village of Chalk which is in any case virtually part of Gravesend now, the rest of Kent to the boundary west of Dartford is almost continuously built-up into a foretaste of Greater London itself. Chalk itself lays its main claim to fame upon the fact that Dickens spent his honeymoon in a cottage in Chalk Road.

Between the A226 and the A2, hemmed in by the paper-making and cement manufacturing industries of the Thameside, and by the chalkpits and gravel workings that pockmark the hinterland, the village of Shorne nevertheless succeeds in being a little haven of quiet on wooded heights overlooking the river and the Essex coast. It is, in fact, one of that select company of Metropolitan Green Belt villages which the 1967 Kent Development Plan named "excepted villages" and decreed that only in the most exceptional circumstances should they be allowed to grow beyond their present boundaries.

In 1777, Richard Hayes of Cobham noted in his diary that from Shorne windmill he could see St Paul's in London with the naked eye. We cannot argue with him; all we can say with certainty is that the view is one feature of Shorne that is lost, perhaps with the loss of the windmill, more probably with the twin additions of atmospheric pollution and intervening development.

A mile outside Shorne village, on the north side of the A226 is Green Farm, near which are the buried remains of the lost village of Merston. This was probably a stockaded Saxon village which, unlike present-day Shorne, was mentioned in the Domesday Survey and then disappeared. Archaeologists in 1957 dug up the foundations of a small Norman church, but the village seems to have been lost to history since 1445.

On the other side of Shorne, there is a large and beautiful belt of woods, including Randall Wood, where there remain traces of Randall Manor house, one of several great houses owned by the de Cobham family, and probably dating from the late thirteenth century.

Alongside the A2, the two villages of Singlewell and Ifield are indistinguishable from the southern extremities of Gravesend but Stone, west of Swanscombe, is prettily placed above the Thames, despite being almost wholly surrounded by the industrial sites that dominate this part of the county.

The parish of Stone has the distinction of playing host to the Kent entrance to the Dartford–Purfleet (Essex) Thames tunnel, and the village is, in fact, the last island of rural North Kent before Dartford reaches out and comes near to closing off the northern half of the parish from the south.

Since Stone is linked with the town of Swanscombe for representation on Kent County Council, we can perhaps cheat a little and slip in a reference to an historical episode in which the Kentish Men take special pride. It was at Swanscombe that, in 1066, the people of Kent won the county motto 'Invicta' (unconquered) by persuading William the Conquerer to grant them the right to perpetuate ancient privileges, including the very old gavelkind custom of dividing inherited land equally among all the sons of a family, instead of passing it all on to the eldest as was the custom elsewhere. This privilege, continued until very recently, was one reason for the very many small holdings scattered throughout the county—and, incidentally, a fruitful source for confusion among later local historians.

The story goes that the Kentish army, fully prepared to fight if necessary, advanced to meet the Normans behind green branches, so that they looked like a marching forest. When they reached the parley site, they dropped the boughs and showed their drawn swords. Rather than do battle, William met their demands. It is a favourite story in West Kent—although in East Kent they tend more often to add the bit about Duke William taking Dover Castle in exchange for his concessions, which puts a slightly different complexion on the incident.

At this point I suggest we double back to look at some of Kent's loveliest countryside and some of its most perfect villages, between the A2–M2 and the North Downs.

It is surprising how many people imagine North Kent to be almost unrelievedly industrial—that includes people from other parts of the county itself. It has to be admitted that there are few more determinedly parochial people than those of Kent. It is common to hear people of the Weald or of Thanet or, for that matter, of North Kent speak as though the whole county were characteristic of that part they happen to know best, but ask them what North Kent is like and they will talk generally of cement factories and papermills as though the glories of the North Downs were somewhere else altogether. It is a pity, for on either side of the three-lane dual carriageway that is this end of the A2, and particularly on the south side, the countryside rears and plunges, up through thickly wooded lanes and down into remote and lovely little valleys as fertile as any in the country.

The *Arethusa* on the river Medway at Upnor


The river Stour at Fordwich

Herne village has been lucky with its conversions of old cottages

**Chestfield Golf Clubhouse welcomes visitors with a picturesque scene**

(*above*) A rare sight in Kent: a thatched cottage at Wingham

(*below*) Landmark for seamen, the ruins of ancient Reculver Church

Chilham: (*top*) old houses line the approach; (*bottom*) the village square

There is a hint of the possibilities of the area at Wilmington, the most north-westerly village in Kent since the 1963 London Government Act created the Greater London Council and threw the London boundaries out beyond Bromley and Bexley. Wilmington village is an extension of Dartford now, but it takes the built-up area out to the edge of acres of orchards and farmland and the parish includes the new settlement on the edge of Joyden's Wood, among the foothills of the Downs. Part of Joyden's Wood is designated as an area of special scientific interest because of some of the plant life to be found there. On the eastern side of Wilmington, is the new development of Hawley wedged against the A225 that links the A2 with the other main highway between London and the Channel Ports, the A20.

South of Wilmington, Hextable is a true village still, although it is closely linked with the town of Swanley. It is a village that has made itself a centre of the market gardening industry in comparatively recent times, and a number of the local residents are of Dutch descent.

The town of Swanley is not to be confused, by the way, with Swanley Village, which although mainly centred around the Darenth Road is capable of rewarding visitors with such little pleasures as the village church. Despite its being not much more than a century old yet, the church is a very pretty little building, attractively sited. Swanley Village is another of those 'excepted villages', deemed to be worth protecting from the worst effects of new growth.

The North Kent orchards enfold the village of Sutton-at-Hone in a cloud of blossom in springtime, giving it something of the appearance of an island in the foam that flows alongside the quiet River Darent. One of the most distinctive features of the Sutton-at-Hone neighbourhood is the old moated house of St Johns Jerusalem, about a quarter of a mile outside the village. This was once one of the Kentish 'commanderies' (the other was at Swingfield, near Dover) of the Knights Hospitallers of the Order of St John of Jerusalem. The manor and the chapel were granted to

D

Sir Michael Dennys by Henry VIII after the dissolution, when the Knights were disbanded. Since then, a series of distinguished owners have included Abraham Hill, a founder of the Royal Society, Kent historian Edward Hasted and, later, Sir Stephen Tallents who presented the house to the National Trust in 1943 but lived on there until he died. Now, the house and the very beautiful gardens are open to the public and are one of the big tourist attractions of this end of the county.

The A225 links up with the A20 at Farningham, and it is that village's misfortune—or, perhaps on second thoughts, its good fortune—that millions of travellers through Kent each year carry away with them an impression of the village founded entirely upon the ribbon development on both sides of the road. A few shops, some undistinguished houses, garages and cafés, all managing to look somehow untidy and uncaring.

In fact, this is not Farningham at all, whatever the signs say. As they do everywhere, the signs refer not to the village, but to the parish boundaries. Farningham was one of the first Kent villages to be by-passed, and to find the modern descendant of the old Saxon village it is necessary to leave the main road and drop down the side of the Darenth Valley into an utterly charming little corner of old Kent. Paths slope sharply down from the village High Street, to the river Darent with its eighteenth-century bridge and the Lion Hotel which was once the village inn and is still a hostelry of some reputation.

Captain Bligh (of the *Bounty*) once lived in the Manor House at Farningham, which was a direct hit casualty during the Second World War. The whole Darenth Valley is rich in archaeological treasures and the grounds of the old Manor House yielded evidence of a first-century Roman house on the site. The oldest remaining buildings in the village, though, are immediately north-west and south-east of the bridge, and the Old Corn Mill on the northern arm of the divided river at this point is a very attractive main feature of one of the village's best groups of buildings.

When the new motor road replaced the old coaching route, an

important part of the economies of the villages was siphoned off. But, inevitably, it was not long before the villages were reaching out mendicant palms behind their backs in the hope of coaxing alms from the new-style travellers and the new roadside commercialism characterizes many of the trunk road villages which, thus, never show their pretty faces to the customers who do not take time to look for them.

The A2 sweeps on its south-westerly way from Farningham roundabout to pass through the steep, wooded Downs-side village of West Kingsdown where the crossroads created the village, most of which lies north of the road, almost wrapped around by the Brands Hatch motor racing track, nearly five hundred feet up into the Downs.

For the most part, the North Downs are wooded, with occasional patches of farmland scooped out of the hillsides and, every now and again, a village creates a foothold on the slopes. Such a village is Fawkham Green, with its village green at one (the southern) end, and the old church of St Mary at the other end.

West of Fawkham is Horton Kirby, another of those 'excepted' Green Belt villages, on the east bank of the river Darent, which has existed on the site since Saxon times and, in fact, may have had its beginnings in Roman days. Certainly, the site of Roman habitation has been excavated just upstream of the village.

South Darenth spreads itself across the railway just outside Farningham Road Station, almost integrated with its closest neighbour, Sutton-at-Hone, but Darenth half-way between the railway and the A2, is a quite large but compact and distinct village on the edge of a large wooded area comprised of Darenth Wood and Lords Wood. This part of Kent has, for centuries, been part of London's countryside, and the manor of Darenth was given by King Athelstan to Duke Eadulf who, in turn, gave the church and the manor to Canterbury Cathedral in 940. Some old dungeons remain in the Elizabethan Clock House in Green Street Green, a small hamlet just south-west of Darenth, which are said to be connected by underground passages to the Old Ship Inn on the other side of the road.

It is difficult to travel far in this part of Kent without being reminded of the industrial plainness among the scenic beauty. But then, round a bend, there are suddenly villages like Bean and Betsham and Southfleet, all of them protected Green Belt villages and all, although not equally, attractive. There were once gunpowder factories at Bean, and Southfleet, just south of the A2 and balancing (in name, if not in size) Northfleet on the other side, with its cottages and its thirteenth-century church. Southfleet is a very old village indeed, mentioned in Domesday, and near the reputed site of the Roman town of Vagniacae.

Longfield and Hartley span the railway almost due south of Swanscombe. They are both modern 'growth' areas, like the new neighbourhoods of New Barn and Istead Rise, both of which are Gravesend 'satellites'. South of Hartley is the controversial 'new village' of New Ash Green.

New Ash Green is generally recognized as a planning mistake. Opinions are divided about whether or not the village plan is a good one, but there is much greater unanimity about the fact that it was allowed to be planted in the wrong place. Originally conceived as a complete new village to be built by one developer, it ran into difficulties when the developer had to pull out without completing the project. The older village of Ash is smaller and rather attractive in a self-effacing way.

Hartley, too, has its old village a little way from the new estates, where it is said Daniel Defoe once lived in a cottage near the Black Lion Inn, and wrote *Robinson Crusoe* while he was there. The diarist John Evelyn, too, had friends in this part of Kent and almost certainly stayed at Hartley or nearby at some time.

The A227 links the A2 outside Gravesend with the A20 at Wrotham. To do so, it courses through Nurstead and Meopham, which for some perfectly acceptable reason, no doubt, is pronounced *Meppam*, and is famed for its cricket matches and for one of the best kept greens in the county. The earliest recorded cricket match at Meopham was played on 10th July 1778, against a Chatham side.

The village has another claim to fame, though. It was in Meopham church, in 1607, that John Tradescant, gardener to Charles I, was married and, a year later, where his son John was christened. They were both much travelled botanists in later years and hundreds—perhaps thousands—of Acacia Avenues all over Britain can be credited directly to the Tradescants, father and son. Among several plants and shrubs which they introduced to the country for the first time were acacia and lilac.

Meopham was selected to become one of London's new satellite towns soon after the end of the Second World War. The plan would have brought 11,000 new homes and 40,000 people to live in them into the area, as well as industries to employ the newcomers. But, much to the relief of the local people at the time, the plan was abandoned. That has not prevented the arrival of new populations to the vicinity, though. Today, an inflated Meopham and Meopham Green sit immediately east of the road, between the big estate-style development around Meopham railway station and the new villages of Vigo among the woods that teeter up to the brink of the sharp drop from the ridge of the Downs, across the old Pilgrims' Way, through Harvel and Culverstone towards Trottiscliffe.

Don't try to guess the local pronunciation of that: it's *Trosley*, and the nearby Trosley Towers new development has adopted the phonetic spelling to distinguish it from the old village, which lies at the bottom of the south slope of the downs. Trottiscliffe church has for a neighbour a farmhouse which is on the site of a medieval palace of the Bishop of Rochester, but the area was inhabited long before that. In the parish, above the village, are the 4,000 years old Coldrum Stones, near the Pilgrims' Way. They are all that remain of a once imposing burial chamber dating from about 2,000 B.C., and they are now National Trust property.

Nearby Birling is a village of great charm, hedged about with a good deal of new building but still showing off many sixteenth- and seventeenth-century houses, picturesque with their half-timbering and plaster, as well as a number of characteristic local ragstone houses of the nineteenth century.

Another of the picturesque villages hereabouts is Ryarsh, a brick-making village tucked away behind the angle formed by the junction of the A228 Rochester Road and the A20.

It was in one of the quarries at Halling that a man's skeleton, surrounded by flint chips and the bones of a horse and sheep were found. They were 25,000 years old and are now in the Museum of the Royal College of Surgeons in London. Bishop Gundolph of Rochester built himself a palace at Halling, but only a short stretch of the wall beside the churchyard remains to remind us of the fact today.

On the opposite bank of the river Medway lies Wouldham, chiefly notable for being the one-time home of Walter Burke, purser of the *Victory*, in whose arms Nelson died at Trafalgar. To this day, schoolchildren in the village commemorate the occasion by placing flowers on the purser's grave on Trafalgar Day, and attending a memorial service in the church.

Wouldham was a small, riverside village right up to the mid-nineteenth century, most of the 250-odd villagers earning their daily bread by farming or lime-burning. It was the coming of the cement industry in the second half of the nineteenth century that brought a population explosion, and several hundred small houses were built for the men and their families who came to support the new industry. When, in 1904, the Wouldham Cement Co. put up the shutters and moved across to Essex, followed between the wars by the Associated Portland Cement Co. works closure, the villagers had to look elsewhere for work and Wouldham lost its main reason for being. It still wears a look of bewildered purposelessness today, as though it has never really recovered from its change of circumstances, although it is certainly no ghost village, and new industries have established themselves in and around Wouldham.

One of the most remote villages in this otherwise comparatively closely settled area is Luddesdown, which seems to have hidden itself away among the wooded hills between Cobham and Halling. Perhaps that very remoteness has contributed to the boast of Luddesdown Court that it is one of the oldest inhabited houses in England, dating from Saxon times. It was certainly owned by Bishop Odo, who probably adapted it from an earlier Saxon house. Not surprisingly, there is much of interest in the house, from wall paintings to graffiti and the little combined bear-pit and dovecote. The house and the nearby church can both be visited by appointment.

The village of Dode has nothing but a tiny church for its memorial. Dode was one of the victims of the Black Death which wiped out whole villages like it in the mid-fourteenth century. All traces of the medieval village are now lost, except the little flint Norman church, hidden away along a lane that is barely more than a track, which sleeps away the centuries in perpetual mourning for its long-lost congregation.

There is nothing remote about Cuxton, which has expanded a great deal in recent years, straggling up from the side of the River Medway to a fairly dense concentration of houses. In 1487 a Lord Mayor of London, Sir William Whorne, built Whorne's Place for his country home at Cuxton. Today, the village is another of the string of cement-making villages, but even before the industry arrived, the lime-burners were busy throughout the Medway valley supplying London builders with lime for mortar from their riverside kilns. Cuxton Hill thrusts up at the north end of the village and from the top there is a fine view across and along the river, spanned a short distance ahead by the two-thirds mile long M2 bridge—a rather spectacular example of beautiful modernity, with spans that were the longest in the world built on the particular cantilever principle used in its design.

If the riverside villages are less than perfectly beautiful, the same cannot be said at all for Cobham, surely one of the gems among the North Downs villages. Cobham was well-known to Dickens and its famous old Leather Bottle Inn was immortalized in *Pickwick Papers* as the place where the lovelorn Tracy Tupman stayed. The village sits on top of a ridge overlooking the slopes where the North Downs play chaperone by keeping apart the valleys of the Thames and the Medway, and so the village displays itself from the opposite slopes. All round are coppices and woodlands, including the great and beautiful park of Cobham Hall, and very rich farming land, fully deserving the Kent Development Plan description of the area as one of great landscape value. The Countryside Commission has named it an area of outstanding natural beauty.

The attractions of Cobham, both economic and visual, no doubt, have been recognized since prehistoric times. There are very old earthworks just north of Cobham Hall, and large sarsen stones are scattered throughout the village. The church is justly famous for its unique collection of about sixty medieval memorial brasses. Owletts, at the west end of the village, is a Charles II house, particularly notable for its contemporary staircase and plaster ceiling, owned by the National Trust and open to the public during the summer.

Outside the village proper, the red brick elegance of Cobham Hall is now a girls' public school. It is one of the largest and best examples of Tudor manor house style building in Kent, standing in fifty acres of superbly landscaped grounds.

Since the war, several big new houses have been built in and around the village, but they fit in well enough and if the Lawrence Drive council houses are, perhaps, a little less in sympathy, at least they are so sited as not to intrude.

A mile south of Cobham, Sole Street's most distinguishing feature is the Yeoman's House, leased to the National Trust now, the Great Hall of which can be visited by appointment.

Another new village is destined to spring up around Walderslade, at present a scattering of homes built, for the most part, between the wars or since the Second World War among the trees and steep slopes of the Downs above the Medway Towns. The Kent Development Plan provides for the area to be acquired by the county council in order to bring the fragmented ownerships into one which can be serviced and developed with homes, shops, schools and other services.

Overlooking the Medway to the north, Hartlip is a very prettily sited little village, with several attractive old houses in the neighbourhood, and a Roman villa site within the parish.

The Downs here are a little less heavily wooded; there are more orchards and open farmland. East of the Medway Towns again, between the A2 and the M2 (which, incidentally, has been called, with some justification, the prettiest motorway in Britain) many of the villages have a cherished look, nestling usually in folds among the great sweep of the north slopes.

Villages like Borden, the approach to which is past some very tastefully designed modern homes and the road bends abruptly round the squat square-towered church with its wooden diamond-shaped clock face. The massive-looking thatched barn beyond the church seems to loom up suddenly and then relent and stand aside to reveal a very eye-catching half-timbered house beside it.

Neighbouring Tunstall beckons any traveller with a spark of poetry in his soul along its approach road, which glories in the name of Heart's Delight Road. It is as pretty as its name, and it leads straight into a very pretty little group of old buildings at the edge of the village. There has been comparatively little modern development here, and in fact, when there were plans to convert an old stable block at Cedar House into modern homes in 1970, the project was turned down on the grounds that it would spoil the village.

Still going south, the road does a rather inconsequential right-angled turn to the left and then, soon afterwards, changes its mind again and does an equally sharply right-angled turn to the right in order to cross over the M2 into Bredgar, which is larger than Tunstall and still growing. Quite a high proportion of newer houses mingle very harmoniously with some of the more traditional village architecture that radiates outwards from the little pond and the war memorial, where they create a wholly delightful picture of traditional rural life.

Milstead's most striking feature is undoubtedly its really rather superb half-timbered Elizabethan manor house which looks across the road through the village at the church opposite. There are other similar houses and cottages, too. The village, like so many along this strip of the Downs, has the M2 at one end of it, but the road underpasses the motorway without any fuss and it is really quite astonishing how often it is possible to cross the motorway without realizing it. When this happens, it can be disorientating to double back and find yourself crossing over the road a second time without being aware of having crossed it in the opposite direction between times.

Nearby Rodmersham has attracted some individualistic modern architecture to its outskirts to rub shoulders, in a very dignified and not too intimate way, with stolidly Georgian yeoman farmhouse neighbours and the crumbly flint of the old church of St Nicholas among its orchards at the northern end of the village.

An artist, invited to draw from memory a typical village centre might well draw Lynsted without knowing it. There is the village pub, the church, and the clustering houses, all perched on top of a hill. At a slightly lower level is a group of characteristic half-timbered houses and a thoroughly picturesque little pond surrounded by some beautiful mature chestnut trees and colonized by geese and ducks. It is altogether an obvious favourite for the title of Kent's Best Kept Village and it comes as no surprise to discover that it won the title for the East Kent small villages in 1967.

Adjoining the parish of Lynsted to the south is the tiny parish of Kingsdown. There is no village, just a few hamlets and farm groups, but there is a very pretty little church of St Catherine, tucked away among the trees above which the rather ornate stone spire reaches up to intrigue travellers on the M2 just to the north. The church lies off the main road, if a secondary road so little used by any but purely local traffic can be so called, at the end of a lane that ends abruptly outside a nicely converted oast, now called Church Oast, whose old square kilns, topped by two white cowls, make a very attractive complement to the church. The church was built as recently as 1875 and is now administered jointly with neighbouring Lynsted, but there was a much older church on the site before the present one was built.

Due south again, and again crossing over the motorway, the road drops down into the centre of Doddington and so invites visitors to miss the church of St John the Baptist, which is hidden away modestly at the side of a lane at one end of the village. That is a pity, because it is a rather charming little building, with a white weatherboarding tower. The rest of the village, which was there for the Domesday Survey, stretches itself along the main street in groups of very pretty little cottages, interspersed with some new houses, and seemingly centred upon the spacious road junction where 'The Chequers' public house dominates the whole village.

Turning north, the road tunnels through the overhang of beech and chestnut into Newnham, rather smaller than Doddington and probably prettier in its smaller scale way, but of a quite distinctly similar pattern. The main street includes Calico House, a timbered Tudor home on the site of an older house, with part of a plaster façade which was added in the eighteenth century.

Back on the A2, Norton is a parish without a village of that name. The nearest to it is Norton Ash, just north of Norton cross-roads, but the most interesting building is probably Norton Court, which is just outside the hamlet of Lewson Street. The house was probably built by Inigo Jones in 1625, and it is in an architectural style more usually associated with the Georgian period which came later. Another lovely old house nearby is Provender, which is also sixteenth century and, in parts, older than that, but is more typical of the period.

Stone is another parish without a village—indeed, without a single resident if the 1971 census can be believed. The parish adjoins Norton and the census disclosure was challenged as soon as it was published but, even so, the total population certainly does not exceed two or three people.

Ospringe straddles the A2 just west of Faversham. In fact, the borough of Faversham reached out and enclosed the village in 1935 and today one of the town's largest council estates is within the original Ospringe parish. But the village retains its old character very bravely, in spite of the effects of modern heavy traffic through its main street, and several attractive old houses huddle together for protection against the intrusion of modernity.

Some of the best of the old houses are in Water Lane, which strikes south at right angles to the A2, past the restored Maison Dieu, once a pilgrims' hostel and now a museum for local bygones and excavated relics of nearby Roman occupation. Until the 1960s, the lane regularly carried a stream between its built-up footpaths out to the watercress beds on the other side of the A2, but now the whole lane is culverted and the water flows beneath the surface—less picturesque but much more convenient for the roadside residents!

Water Lane leads past the old timbered Queen Court farmhouse, a reminder that for many years the manor of Ospringe was owned by the queens of England after Henry III granted it to trustees as part of the dowry of his intended Queen Eleanor. Just past Queen Court, on the edge of the farm's hop gardens, is the little church of SS Peter and Paul, of Norman origin but with a modern and unusual ridge-roofed tower in which the bells are mounted in two tiers.

Immediately south of the M2 but still part of Ospringe parish is the former hamlet of Painters Forstal, now almost large enough, since the addition of a small estate of council houses, to be called a village with its own tiny pub, 'The Alma', and village stores.

# 3

# Thanet and North-East Kent

THANET is the parson's nose of Kent, turned up from the rump of the Channel coast, and bristling with a few determined-looking whiskers of trees and power-cable pylons.

It is a flat, almost wholly featureless landscape that the Isle of Thanet spreads before the thousands of foreign tourists who arrive at the Pegworth Bay hoverport every year, giving little hint of the lush richness of the soil which has made this one of the major market gardening and vegetable growing areas of the south-east. Too exposed for orchards or hops, and too dry for pasture, Thanet presents an almost unique landscape for Kent, with about 15 per cent of the farming land given over to cereals and almost all the rest to such vegetables as cabbages, cauliflower and potatoes.

There is an almost complete lack of hedges here, too—a feature of the county's agriculture that has become fairly widespread since the Second World War, as farmers have taken advantage of increased mechanization which operates at its most economically efficient on large areas of uninterrupted land. But in Thanet, the hedges have been long gone; since they were grubbed out during the Napoleonic wars as a defensive measure in case of invasion. No-one has ever thought it necessary to replace them.

No longer an island, the Wantsum channel that made the name well-deserved five hundred years ago is today little more than a ditch across the marshlands it has left behind.

It was at Thanet that the Roman invaders first stepped ashore on British soil; here they made their first base, on a little island which they called Rutupiae, at the southern end of the Wantsum channel, at that time a navigable waterway a mile wide between the Isle of Thanet and the rest of Kent. The Roman occupation of Britain lasted four hundred years, and one of the earliest memorials to their stay remains today in the great walls of Richborough Castle, outside Sandwich.

It was to the Isle of Thanet, too, that the Jutish pirate chieftains, Hengist and Horsa, brought their invasion force in 449. Their memorial flies over the county today—the rampant white horse, said to have originated as the county emblem from the device of Horsa, which he may have carried painted upon his shield.

They have another memorial, too: in 1949, a crew of Danes brought a 1500th anniversary reminder of that invasion in the shape of a replica of the old longship, the *Hugin*, which now stands on the cliff above Pegwell Bay, its dragon head mouth agape and its sides lined with replicas of the shields of those early fore-runners of the tourists who arrive in England from the cross-Channel hoverports. But perhaps their greatest memorial is the English nation itself, for it was the Jutes who laid the foundations of that federation of kingdoms that was eventually to become the United Kingdom of today.

Neither the Romans nor the Jutes were welcomed whole-heartedly when they arrived at the Thanet coastline. St Augustine and his little band of monks, who stepped ashore in much the same place, at least came in peace, to convert Britain to the new Christian faith. His 'invasion' was to last for 2,000 years and his memory is enshrined in the dedications of dozens of Kent churches built long after his death. Today, a cross marks the spot where he was received by King Ethelbert of Kent and invited to deliver his first sermon in England, at Ebbsfleet, where local legend endows a stone, upon which the saint is said to have stepped (and upon which, later, St Mildred is said to have placed her foot) with the ability to fly back to its original spot should anyone move it away from there.

In the years following these three historical milestones, history treated Thanet very lightly indeed. No industries grew up here as they did, for example, in the Weald in the great days of iron and wool. Margate and Ramsgate were mere fishing villages for centuries until the Industrial Revolution (which meant very little to Thanet in any direct sense) made possible railway outings to the seaside. Then the two towns boomed into importance as the two principal Kent coastal resorts and soon thousands of trippers, most of them from London, were filling the hotels and boarding houses and baring their legs (a little more each year!) to the sands and the seas around the Thanet coastline.

Many of the trippers came back, year after year, and brought their children until the towns became holiday extensions of the family home. When 'old 'uns' retired, they recalled the happy days on the Margate sands and looked for a home where they could live out their lives remembering and enjoying the good sea air. In that way, the Thanet resorts and the 'satellite' resorts that grew up all along the north east Kent coastline, became characterized not only as holiday resorts but also as places to which to retire. Today, the highest concentrations of pensioners and over-80s are found in this part of the county.

But although the towns are quite densely populated, the Thanet hinterland is not. There is an almost empty look about it and the villages are small and well separated in a way that is reminiscent of Romney Marsh, although the two landscapes are completely different.

The Thanet resorts now form an almost continuous built-up area right round the island's coastline. Inside this crescent-shaped area, almost completely surrounded by it yet still just identifiably separate, St Peter's (Broadstairs) boasts a church that protects the memory if not the substance of that Richard Joy who was known as the Kentish Samson for his feats of strength, performed before no less an audience than King William II himself.

These feats included a tug-o'-war with an "extraordinarily strong horse" and, in 1669, lifting from the ground a stone weighing 2,240 pounds—an achievement that springs into meaningfulness (not to say scepticism) when you remember that the present weightlifting world record is round about the 890 pounds mark. Joy died in 1742 and was buried in St Peter's churchyard.

Like some of the Romney Marsh villages, several of the Thanet communities have declined, because of geographical changes over the years, from being thriving towns and ports. While the Wantsum remained open to waterborne traffic, for instance, Minster was a busy port. Today, it is chiefly notable for its parish church of St Mary, sometimes called the Thanet Cathedral, which has a massive Norman tower with a look-out in the south corner. It is Thanet's oldest and loveliest church, said to be built on the site of St Mary's Convent, which was founded about A.D. 670. About seventy years later, a larger convent was built further inland, which did not, however, protect it from marauding Danes in 840, when it was burned.

After that, it was not rebuilt until the twelfth century, and it was not until 1937 that a small group of Benedictine nuns from St Walburga's Abbey in Bavaria quietly brought the monastic life back to Minster, although their Abbey is not the original one, but a nearby twelfth-century building. In 1970, an orgy of destruction, blamed at the time on practitioners of black magic, caused damage to the font and to statues, vestments and fabrics of St Mary's church.

Cleve Court at Minster was bought by Lord Carson in 1920. He was a lawyer and politician who died in 1935, and his widow lived on there until she, too, died in 1966. While she lived, Lady Carson was convinced that the house was haunted by a Grey Lady, who had a habit of appearing when children were in the house. She was said to be the spirit of the wife of a tyrannical former owner who kept her childless and locked in her room.

Despite its position on the threshold of England, Thanet is not all ancient and historic. North of Minster, Acol is a village with

The agricultural college, Wye

Pithead winding gear at Tilmanstone in the Kent Coalfield

Ham Church

The Old Mill House at Westwell

The village centre, Charing

(*above*) One of Kent's prettiest village greens at Hernhill

(*left*) A thatched roof on the thirteenth-century Southdown Cot Nonington

virtually no history at all. Even the church there is less than a hundred years old, converted at the end of the nineteenth century from the school that it was until then. Now the village has a large caravan site.

You have to be looking for Manston in order to find it at all, in spite of the fact that it advertises itself with an airfield. This was one of the famous Battle of Britain fields and later, after the war, it was an RAF air-sea rescue helicopter station. Now it is an RAF training field, with a small aircraft museum. The airfield wraps the little village from which it takes its name in such a way that all roads seem to pass the field but never lead to the village. In fact, though, determined explorers who do find it discover a pleasant little place of mainly modern homes laid out with a feeling for space and comfort, and with all the characteristic sense of aloofness common to most of the Thanet villages.

A golf course does its best to prevent Birchington from running into Westgate-on-Sea, which long ago ran into Margate and gave the town an almost unbroken six miles or so of seafront. But Birchington will continue to look like a village all the time it still has its square in front of the pub, and its old buildings—like the fifteenth-century Olde Cottage on the approach to the Thanet Way.

Nearby Quex Park, with its popular Powell-Cotton Museum and its secretive little private chapel revealed among the trees by the delicate ironwork of the spire that caps it, attracts a great many visitors every year. The chapel was built purposely by a former owner so that he could indulge his love of campanology (or change-ringing, as its practitioners call it) with estate employees. The museum itself contains an enormous variety of trophies and mementoes of the big game hunting days of Major Percy Powell-Cotton, all displayed in cases and cabinets, including tableaux of African wildlife in naturalistic surroundings, and a full range of native African weaponry as well as European hunters' guns of all kinds. The fire-arms collection includes a number of cannon out on the terrace, including one which is reputed to have

E

been used during the French Revolution. The museum is open one day a week, and is well worth a visit, as much for the attractions of the surrounding parkland as for the interest of the exhibits inside the house. A member of the Crispe family of Quex Park during the Commonwealth period unwillingly helped towards the restoration of the monarchy. Henry Crispe was kidnapped by Thanet Royalist Capt Golding, and shipped to Flanders where he was held for eight months until £3,000 ransom was paid towards the funds of the king's supporters.

Birchington's church is distinguished by having the great Italian poet and painter, Dante Gabriel Rossetti, buried in the churchyard. He died in 1882, having chosen to spend the last days of his life in Kent, and his memorials are a stained glass window and a cross in the churchyard.

The village of Monkton had two churches when the Domesday Survey was made. Today there is only one, but that has outside it the only village stocks remaining in Kent, so perhaps that is some compensation to the village for the loss of its other church. Several of the houses in the village and the surrounding parish are of Tudor origin, and we know that this part of Thanet was occupied by the Anglo-Saxons because when in 1971, gas pipelines were being laid across fields outside the village, bones, pottery, brass and glass of that period were uncovered.

Another of the Wantsum ports was Sarre, now on the main Canterbury–Thanet road and three miles from the nearest sea. The Wantsum is still there, though—a poorly-looking stream that slips under the road almost unnoticed.

Sarre is not even a large village today. But it is an attractive enough place, with its reminders of visits by Charles Dickens (among a regular 'Who's Who' of celebrities) to the Crown Inn, once a posting house and now famous for its own, made-on-the-premises cherry brandy, made to a recipe handed down from a seventeenth-century Huguenot refugee landlord who presumably brought it with him from the Netherlands.

A writer in the early eighteenth century referred to a church at Sarre, but it seems to be the only reference to it and no trace has ever been found of the building. All sorts of explanations have been offered for this, the most likely being that the author's notes became confused and the church to which he referred when he wrote about Sarre was actually in another village altogether. In its day as a port, Sarre stood on the Thanet side of the principal ferry operating between the island and the Kentish mainland.

Another Wantsum ford was at St Nicholas-at-Wade—as the name suggests. The church, which bears the marks of Norman handiwork, is a rather fine one, as befitted the importance of the place when the church was built. Now it looks down benevolently upon a little group of modern flatlets for elderly residents.

Elsewhere in the village, though, there is an almost Dutch look about some of the older houses. St Nicholas' Court, which recalls the Georgian period in which it was built, still has an underground chapel cut into the chalk, which was supposed to have been used by the Lollards, those fourteenth–fifteenth century religious re-formers who supported John Wycliffe, and whose teachings pre-pared the way for the Reformation. The word Lollard is derived from a Dutch word meaning 'to sing in a low voice', and the fact that St Nicholas-at-Wade was a Lollard stronghold no doubt accounts for the Dutch influence in the local architecture.

On the mainland side of the Wantsum, the Chislet marshes retain the watercourse character they have had for centuries, but the village of Chislet played host to the outriders of the Kent coal mining industry when it became the northernmost of the county's coal villages. The colliery at Chislet was closed in 1970, and already the slagheaps (with some help from the National Coal Board) are well integrated into the local landscape, with trees and undergrowth blurring the normally assertive outlines of these man-made hills.

There is a local legend that Chislet once had a hamlet priest who was never seen by his parishioners, from whom he received food in return for his blessing given from a small window they could not see into. The church at Chislet is Norman, possibly on the site of a Saxon church, with an odd little spire that looks as though it were made for a much smaller church. Nearby hamlets include Chislet Forstal, Marshside, Highstead and Boyden Gate.

Back on the A28 Canterbury–Thanet road is Upstreet and Grove Ferry, where there was once a flourishing industry introduced by a local man who grew lavender along the riverside and distilled perfume from it. Today, Grove Ferry is a popular spot with visitors to an attractive area between the Great Stour at Grove Ferry itself and the Little Stour just south of the ferry.

Hersden is another mining village on the East Kent coalfield and just off the A28, overlooking the Stour Valley and the lake-land landscape created by the local gravel extraction industry, Westbere delights its visitors with old timbered houses, thatched cottages and barns, and a black and white Tudor inn.

Until quite recently, Westbere was one of the few remaining places in England where the traditional bread and cheese feast for the poor of the parish was perpetuated, and the church has some mid-seventeenth-century books that throw interesting light upon the local poor rate and the churchwardens' accounts.

Northwards, Hoath lies in thickly wooded countryside some two miles from the sea behind Herne Bay. It was here that Archbishop Thomas Cranmer and Bishop of London Nicholas Ridley stayed, at the old Tudor manor house at Ford, when they revised the "Thirty Nine Articles". Cranmer was arrested at Hoath.

The North Kent coastline, west from the Thanet resorts, has a desolate, who-could-love-me? look, especially at low tide, when the pebbly mud gleams glumly between the sea wall and the petulant waterline. There is scarcely a sign of human habitation all the way from Birchington to Herne Bay.

One place that interrupts this blank-faced desolation is Reculver, where the second half of the twentieth century has created a caravan township and grafted on to the native sobriety of the spot a somewhat forced air of seaside gaiety that does constant battle with the spoil-sport gusts that come ashore here after a practically uninterrupted sweep down from the North Pole.

Excavation of the site of the Roman fortress at Reculver has been going on steadily since 1951, and has uncovered a barracks and a bath house and other relics of the Roman occupation of the site. The original church at Reculver was probably founded by Egbert, King of Kent in about 670, but the two towers that now identify Reculver from afar date from the twelfth century, when the old Saxon church there was enlarged. It is said that the towers were modelled upon those of Davington Priory, near Faversham, and the story tells how one prioress of Davington was travelling to Broadstairs by sea accompanied by her sister, when they were wrecked in a storm off Reculver. The prioress was saved, and as a gesture of thanks for her deliverance, as well as by way of a memorial to her sister, who was drowned, she had the twin towers built as a navigational aid and a warning to seamen of the dangers of the coast at this point. This is no more than a legend, but the towers certainly became known to seamen as 'The Sisters', and after the church fell into disrepair and was partly dismantled in the 1800s by parishioners who vandalized it for the stone, wood and lead, Trinity House bought and afterwards maintained the remains as an aid to shipping.

Closing in on Herne Bay, the little cluster of houses and caravans at Hillborough just about allows the village to retain its separate identity, which is more than can be said for Beltinge, now as indistinguishable from the urban density of the town's east side as Greenhill is on the west. The only real difference is that while Beltinge started out as a distinct village, well clear of old Herne Bay, Greenhill is an almost completely modern estate-type development.

South of Herne Bay, on the Canterbury Road, is the attractive village of Herne, with an unusually picturesque group of old buildings at its centre, opposite the church, which have been very sensitively restored and decorated. The village is fortunate enough to have a flourishing conservation society of its own, which has restored the two hundred year old Herne Mill, a large and typically Kentish smock mill which has overlooked the village since it replaced an older post mill on the same site in the sixteenth century. Milling is still carried out on at the mill which, however, uses electricity today.

In 1626 the will of a certain Mr Thomas Hole of Ash-next-Sandwich left 13s. 4d. a year 'forever', part of which was for the Herne bell ringers if they rang the church bells on St Thomas' Day (21st December) each year, in commemoration of the time he was lost in Blean Forest and found his way back to civilization again by following the sound of the bells of St Martin's Church.

There is a comparatively short stretch of open coastline between Herne Bay and the first hint of approaching Whitstable, which is Swalecliffe. At the end of the Second World War, this was a small estate-type development village tacked on to the very much older group of buildings around St. John's Church, where farmland ended abruptly at the edge of the crumbling clay cliff and the encroaching shingle of the beach. Today the village arcs in a deep crescent at the middle of which is the railway station; houses have almost completely taken over the farmland and very nearly meet up with the virtually independent village of caravans on the marshes at the eastern point of the crescent.

Westward, Swalecliffe melts imperceptibly into Tankerton which has long ago lost any real separate identity having become a sea-front extension of the residential periphery of Whitstable itself.

On the other side of the railway line and the Thanet Way, is a village of a quite different character, Chestfield. Its fine hillside golf course is the dominating feature, and the village has retained the air of being a well-to-do bit of Whitstable countryside, with some really very beautiful genuinely old houses, some very charming but not so genuinely old houses, and a lot of unassumingly modern development, most of which nevertheless, looks as though it has managed to settle in fairly comfortably with the much more old-established neighbours.

South of Chesterfield, the roads switchback up into the Blean Forest that still characterizes much of the resoundingly named parish of St Cosmus and St Damian in the Blean. Today, Blean

Woods and the adjoining Dunkirk Woods are all that remain of the former royal forest of Blean. Luckily, the remnant may well continue in its present state for a long time, protected as it is by the Nature Conservancy as an area of special scientific interest because of its wealth of bird, plant and insect life.

The road passes through the village of Blean, a scattering of comparatively modern houses along the main road, with the church that gives the parish its name and, incidentally, which is one of only three churches in all England that could do so. Both the others are in Sussex. The church at Blean is the only real reminder of the age of the village. It dates from the Early English period, although it was restored in 1866. At the southern end of the village, the land drops abruptly down into Canterbury and there is a magnificent view from the top of Honey Hill over the wooded slopes towards the Cathedral.

Across country, eastwards, the line of the old Canterbury–Whitstable railway line, the first passenger-carrying line in the world, can still be picked out here and there; although the metals are gone, the cuttings are still recognizable.

Skirting the cubist buildings of the University of Kent at Canterbury (to give it its full name), the city itself now embraces the former separate village of Hackington which, in spite of all the new building on this side of the city, has clung to its village green and the old village pub, 'Ye Olde Beverlie' whose first occupant was the parish clerk. The house was built for him and he turned it into an alehouse from which he was in the habit of selling beer to members of the congregation as they left the church after services.

The eastward route out of Canterbury, going towards Thanet and Sandwich wanders a bit to serve Broadoak before swinging back on course at Sturry, which sits at a point where the main road traffic from Thanet and from Herne Bay meet to go on into Canterbury. The Romans knew it as the place where the Canterbury road met the road to Reculver—Durovernum Cantiacorum and Regulbium. The main feature of Sturry village today is the manor house with its Tudor brick gateway and medieval tithe barn, once the home of Lord Milner, when he was Secretary of State for England, and now owned by King's School, Canterbury.

Just past Sturry, off the main road where it would be tragically easy to by-pass it and never know what you had missed, is Fordwich, the one-time busy port of Canterbury to which the Caen stone that built the Cathedral was brought nine hundred years ago, to be unloaded at the quay which is still there.

Despite its size, Fordwich was important enough to rank with the proud boroughs of Kent from the end of the thirteenth century right up to 1833. It had its own manor, and the smallest town hall in England, which was rebuilt in 1555; it was a member of the Cinque Port of Sandwich, and had a ducking stool. The ducking stool is still there, over the River Stour, to remind passers-by just how far women's lib. has progressed in the past few centuries.

That "compleat angler" Izaak Walton knew of the fame of the river Stour at Fordwich, where the trout were said to be the largest in England, and almost as large as salmon.

The Great Stour wanders across Westbere Marshes, by-passing Stodmarsh, which is being a little presumptuous to line itself up alongside villages much more entitled to the description. However, it is a pert little place, craning up from the marshes themselves on a small hill that washes its feet in the Great Stour, to the north and the Little Stour to the south and which is reputed to derive its name from 'stud marsh', which in turn derived from the practice of the monks of Canterbury who kept their brood mares hereabouts.

One of the gems of this part of Kent is Wickhambreaux, which stands on the banks of the Little Stour, the reason for the tall weather-boarded mill that is one of the features of the waterside village green. The village is helped to fulfil its role of showpiece by the virtual absence of through traffic, as much as by the village green and the nicely scaled fifteenth-century church and neighbouring buildings.

The 'local' at Wickhambreaux is the Hooden Horse Inn, the name of which hints at the lingering in these parts of the old East Kent and Thanet custom of hoodening, which may date from Saxon times. The hooden horse still performs with local Morris dancers: a fairly fearsome wooden horse's head with a hinged lower jaw that can be made to click-clack sharply by the capering 'rider', who plays a somewhat random part in the Morris dances. Quite what was the origin of the hooden horse is not known, although it is widely believed that it is pre-Christian and probably a feature of Woden worship, for which there are other scraps of evidence in this extreme north-eastern corner of the county.

A T-shaped High Street at Wingham, wide and tree-lined, forms the village core, but is hidden by the surrounding wooded slopes until the last moment of approach from every direction, so that it seems to spring into the traveller's path with a flourish that commands attention. The Romans used the spur on which Wingham stands for a crossing point of the river valley by their Canterbury–Richborough road, and the village is still essentially a one-street place on either side of the modern Canterbury–Sandwich road. This has exposed it to a good deal of twentieth century heavy traffic, although the village has been able to cling to its old character by avoiding a lot of modern estate-style new buildings. Nevertheless, there are two small estates built during the 1960s, which fit in quite well with the essential character of the village.

Although the village itself hides away among the trees, the distinctive green spire of its church cannot; it provides an unmistakable landmark from every direction. The Red Lion Inn dominates the whole village streetscape with its thirteenth-century massiveness—for a long time the inn dominated the village in another sense, too, for it was here that local lawgivers used to meet in a big room which served them as a court room in which to hear local pleas.

Preston is more distinguished for what was there than for what is there now. St Mildred's Church is some little distance outside the village, but the village claims that under the water of the pond between Preston Court (which is about 150 years old) and the

Canterbury–Wingham road, are the remains of a palace, once the home of Juliana de Leybourne, Infanta (Princess) of Kent—so-called because she was one of the wealthiest mid-fourteenth-century Kentish landowners, and not because of any claim to royal descent. She died in 1367 and if the palace ever was on the spot where the pond now is, there is no trace of it to be seen today.

Not far from Preston, and within the parish of the same name, is a rather attractive little village, Elmstone. It has a small twelfth-century church, to which the belfry was added some two hundred years later. The font is made of Bethersden marble, and local legend claims that the prayer desk in the church was made from the timbers of a ship which was wrecked in the Wantsum while bringing a priest from Minster to take a service at the church. The priest was saved and the prayer desk was given to the church as a thanks offering for his deliverance.

By crossing the Stour at Pluck's Gutter, a little hamlet at the point where the river divides into the Great and Little Stours, you arrive at the twin villages of West and East Stourmouth, once appropriately named, but now well inland. Stourmouth was yet another of the old Wantsum ports, and the church of All Saints claims to be the second oldest parish church in the country, with foundations dating back to pre-Norman Conquest times. Today, whatever distinction the past gave it, Stourmouth is a quiet agricultural and wholly rural village, completely typical of the Thanet countryside in which it sits.

There is an uncharacteristic litter of hamlets skirting the southern edge of Ash Level; hamlets with names like Cop Street, Ware, Goldstone and Paramour Street (a name to conjure with, if ever there was one!). About two hundred years ago, archaeologists uncovered a Saxon cemetery at Guilton, from which jewellery and weapons and some pottery relics of Saxon domesticity were taken and lodged in Liverpool museum.

And then, at Ash-next-Sandwich (to give it the name that distinquishes it from other villages with the same name in Kent), there is another rather fine glimpse of old Kent in the little group of buildings that includes the half-timbered Chequers Inn, the old Chequers bakery, and Cape House. The tall, slim spire of Ash church is another of those navigational aids for seamen and it used to be repaired with the help of Trinity House, although the village is a good four miles from the sea these days. The parish of Ash was once noted for having twelve manors as well as Richborough Castle within its boundaries. Today there are only five of those manors remaining, but the castle remains are still there. Chequer Court, timbered and moated, is fifteenth century; nearby is Molland, and Paramour Grange has a painted room commemorating the stay there of James I early in the seventeenth century. Another attractive remnant of those twelve manors is Wingham Barton at nearby Westmarsh.

Richborough is the oldest harbour in Kent. The island that is Richborough stands above the marshes as an outcrop of Thanet sand, and it was occupied by the legions of the Emperor Claudius in A.D. 43. For 350 years after that, it was the premier trading and military Channel port of England. It was also one of the last Roman strongholds in Britain, as well as one of the first footholds of Christianity when it was visited by Augustine and his mission in 597.

During the First World War, Richborough operated as a 'ghost' port, all very hush-hush, supplying the British Expeditionary Force in France, and in the 1930s it was pressed into service as a housing site for Jewish refugees from Germany. It was mobilized again during the Second World War, and part of the D-Day Mulberry Harbour was assembled there. In the present decade, there have been plans for a kiss of life investment in a new leisure marina there. But the biggest boost to the area came with the building of the Richborough power station, which looms on the plains-like landscape of Thanet an unmistakable landmark.

The ruins of Richborough Castle are famous as some of the most impressive Roman remains in Britain. This was the Roman Rutupiae, and the great wall that remains is some twenty-five feet high, of flint and tile, surrounding the foundation of some completely lost but clearly once impressive monument—perhaps even a rival of the fabulous Collosus of Rhodes.

Just outside Sandwich, Great Stonar remains at some distance from the original site to remind us of the now completely vanished village that was once a rival port to Sandwich itself. Originally on an island in the Wantsum channel, it was closely linked with the Cinque Ports, but the town vanished during the second half of the fourteenth century, probably destroyed by French raiders. After years of conjecture about its exact whereabouts, this has now been established, at least in part, by excavation, the story of which is told in a corner exhibition at the Powell-Cotton Museum at Quex Park, Birchington.

The whole coastline between Deal and Pegwell Bay is taken up by three very fine golf courses: Prince's, Royal St George's and, south of Sandwich Bay Estate, the Royal Cinque Ports.

# 4

## *East Kent*

WHEN the Redcliffe–Maud commission was considering the re-organization of local government at the end of the 1960s, it was the suggestion of that commission that Kent should be divided into two parts for administrative purposes, with a separate East Kent (and part of East Sussex) county based on Ashford. In the event, what became known as the Maud Report was finally exiled as a result of the change of government that followed the 1970 General Election, and there was a strong Kent lobby—particularly strong in East Kent, which is not altogether surprising—that pressed for the idea of partition to be resurrected. All sorts of arguments were found to support the idea, and there are plenty of people in East Kent to this day who will assure anyone who will listen to them that the Government made a great mistake in not dividing the county.

Well, government decisions are made to give us something to grumble into our beer about, and I might as well disclose myself as one of those who never did think any such division could be realistic. Too much of East Kent is agricultural, with a comparatively low rate yield. The concentrated wealth of Kent is on the western side of the Medway, among the Kentish Men and although there are, of course, ways in which this imbalance could have been offset, the government and I agreed (for once) that one Kent made better sense than two.

But if Kent ever did succumb to the old Kentish Men and Men of Kent division, I suppose the cathedral at Canterbury would continue to look down its tower at the little vanities of men, and out over the pastoral acres of its immediate neighbourhood, and see that nothing was changed for all the arguments, and all the lines on the maps.

These are the acres that foreign visitors to Kent know best. They are the acres they probably see first, and surely remember best. For whether they land at Dover and take the A2 or at Folkestone and travel by the A20, it will be the gentle switchback of farmland and woods and panoramic views punctuated by attractive villages that welcomes them to England's very green and very pleasant land, and they will understand why we call this the Garden of England.

Canterbury itself is like the hub of a wheel, from which the roads radiate in all directions. The A28 strikes off north-east into Thanet and south towards Ashford; the A257 heads practically due east for Sandwich; and the A2 swerves in a southern by-pass round the city on its way between Dover and London.

West of Canterbury, the A2 quickly buries itself in the North Kent countryside, but not really before it has climbed up out of the old city and taken a last look back at the fine view of the cathedral from the little village of Harbledown. This was where pilgrims of old got their first good look at their goal, perhaps from the well to which the Black Prince gave his name when he passed this way. The village is very small, its church faced by the old leper hospital founded by Archbishop Lanfranc in 1084, rebuilt in 1674 and now almshouses.

Further west, at the highest point between Faversham and Canterbury, Dunkirk sits on top of Boughton Hill. The little church, opposite the village school, does not dominate the skyline as it might be expected to. That role is filled by the single steel latticework mast that is part of the wartime radar network and now forms a link in the national 'early warning' system.

But Dunkirk has a more worthy, if less obvious, claim to notice in the geographical chance that puts it just twenty miles from each of nine major Kent towns—Maidstone, Deal, Margate, Hythe, Chatham, Folkestone, Ramsgate, Dover and Sheerness.

It was in the Dunkirk woods that Sir William Courtenay (otherwise John Nichols Thom) fought his last battle in 1838, six years after he stood as Parliamentary candidate for Canterbury, and one year after he proclaimed himself the Messiah and raised a private army of about a hundred simple farm labourer disciples. He shot a constable who was sent to arrest him, and an officer of the troops who came to put down his little insurrection, before he shot himself and several of his followers in Bossenden Wood. The uprising was all over the lack of a church in Dunkirk and sad little incident that it was, it was not altogether in vain, as the present Dunkirk church witnesses to this day.

The reputed grave of 'Mad Thom' is in the churchyard of one of the most prettily situated churches in Kent, at Hernhill. Here, high on the Downs, from where there is an uninterrupted view over the steeply sloping orchards down to the Swale, the Isle of Sheppey, and the Thames and Medway estuary beyond, the church forms one side of the charming little village green. The other sides are formed by the old almshouses and the village inn and farm buildings alongside the orchards. But, in the churchyard, Thom's grave is unmarked for fear of desecration, remembered only by local lore now.

The A28 leaves Canterbury through the parish of Thanington Without, in which the little hamlet of Milton has its tiny, restored church and where the Georgian mansion of Tonford Manor was built from the remains of a fourteenth-century fortified manor house. Much of the church is, in fact, seven hundred years old, and there is a fifteenth-century brass monument to Thomas Halle.

Chartham and Chartham Hatch straddle the road, one on either side. To the south, Chartham climbs up into the spectacularly wooded Chartham Downs; a pretty village, grouped round the green in front of its thirteenth-century church, which incidentally claims the oldest set of five bells in Kent, as well as a memorial brass to a Crusader dated 1306. Chartham paper mill is the descendent of a mill that has worked in Chartham for more than two hundred years, and which is today the world's leading producer of tracing paper.

Northwards, Chartham Hatch is on the route of the old Pilgrim's Way, and other hamlets in the parish are Shalmsford Street and Horton, where a fourteenth-century chapel is now used as a farm building.

The road passes south of Old Wives Lees, but there is no point in diverting to visit the village in the hope of seeing the traditional races, because, like many other traditions they have died out. Races? Oh, yes. For two hundred years it was a tradition of the village for two youths and two maidens to run a race each year for a prize endowed by Sir Dudley Digges. The long barrow at the bottom of Julliberrie Downs is still to be found, however, just down the lane leading to the main Canterbury road. Whose burial site the barrow is, nobody knows, but whoever lies there certainly rests in peace in this lovely part of Kent.

One of the most-visited villages in all Kent is Chilham. Some writers put it at the head of their list of the most attractive villages in the county, but that is being too harsh on too many of the others. Chilham is certainly among the first half-dozen, though.

High above the Stour valley, between Godmersham and Canterbury, Chilham is undeniably a little gem of a village, with its square surrounded by picturesque timber and plaster or old weathered brickwork of Jacobean and Tudor houses, which nudge the keep of the castle on one side and the church on the other. There is one particularly fine old Jacobean house built by Inigo Jones for Sir Dudley Digges, who is buried in the church, and who first recorded the remains of Roman building beneath the castle keep. Certainly the castle dates from Saxon times and was probably a Roman stronghold before that. It was sacked by the Danes, but that, of course, was long before it was given by Henry VIII to Sir Thomas Cheyney when he was Lord Warden of the Cinque Ports. When Sir Thomas left Chilham to go to live on the Isle of Shep-

One of the 'wonders' of Kent: the ancient carved doorway at Bar. freston Church

Once an important town, Eastry keeps its dignity today

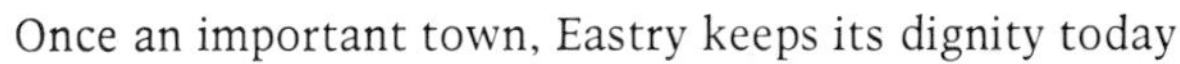

'Folly' and private home: Hadlow Castle

Hop picking at Bettringe

The main street, Biddenden

Part of the gardens at Sissinghurst Place

pey, some of the castle walls went with him to help build his new home there. Now the home of Viscount Masserene and Ferrard, the gardens (which were modified by Capability Brown) contain some of the first wisteria ever to be planted in England.

In 1973, the Battle of Britain Museum, formerly at Langley near Maidstone, was moved to Chilham Castle, where it is now on display, an interesting and occasionally grim reminder that it was over the slumbering acres of Kent that much of the Battle was fought and won in 1940. South of the village, Chilham Park invites the traveller down into neighbouring Godmersham Park. Chilham, in fact, is in a high spot of the county in more senses than one: it is *all* downhill to the neighbours.

Chilham village lies almost in the apex of the triangle formed by the junction of the A252 and the A28 roads. The A252 is the Maidstone road, skirting south of some of the most dense orchard land in all Kent. Among the orchards are villages like Shottenden and Selling, which was known to prehistoric Downslanders, and where a large number of attractive medieval and later houses remain as evidence that its popularity survived to the present time.

The Faversham–Ashford road (A251) slips past the quiet little village of Sheldwich, with its wide green expanse of the Lees, beyond which is another Inigo Jones house, Lees Court, family home of the Earls Sondes. The original house was destroyed by fire in 1910, but was rebuilt in the original style.

In this part of the country, all the signposts seem to have but one object: to make sure you know that Throwley is over there. Over where? Ah, that's their little secret! Throwley is surely one of the most discreet little villages imaginable and trying to find it can be a thoroughly frustrating adventure. But perseverance will eventually disclose it: a little group of half-timbered cottages high in the Downs that seem to have little to do now but remember the time when Sir Thomas Sondes founded the sixteenth-century school there.

Lower down is the beautiful Belmont Park, part of which is one

F

of Kent's most delightful golf courses, and which surrounds the stately home of Lord Harris.

Eastling forms a nucleus for a very intensively farmed area— a fairly undistinguished village, despite being able to claim that it was the birthplace of the celebrated Kent historian, Edward Hasted.

Badlesmere and Leaveland dangle from the Faversham–Ashford road like the twin yolks of a single egg, one on either side. The fifteenth-century black and white timbered Leaveland Court is now a farmhouse.

Further west, at the highest point in the old Swale rural district (now, of course, extinguished and absorbed into the new Swale district, of which it remains, nevertheless, the high spot) is Stalisfield, where the surrounding woodlands surge to a height of more than 600 feet, and the air is still sweet with the scents that the Downsmen have loved for thousands of years.

All this part of Kent is officially recognized as an area of outstanding natural beauty. The villages are many, but nearly all are small and many of them are not compact and easily definable like the Mid-Kent or Weald villages. Charing is not such a village, though. Charing is almost wholly parcelled up into the triangle formed by the A252 splitting off from the A20, which gives the place a neat, well-defined look. The village has been identified with the Roman settlement of Durolenum. More certainly, it was one of the resting places of Henry VIII and his entourage on the way to the Field of the Cloth of Gold in France to meet the Emperor Charles V. And there is no doubt, either, that there was once an Archbishop's palace at Charing, because the remains are still to be found near the church.

For its particular distinguishing feature, Little Chart has chosen to claim the earliest hop garden in all England. It does not always do to inquire too closely into some of these local claims, but as far as I know this particular one is not counter-claimed by any rival, so there seems to be no harm in letting it stand.

An attractive little Stour-side village, the neighbouring hamlet of Little Chart Forstal, with its cossetted miniature green and surrounding houses and buildings on the very edge of the high ground that slopes away northwards and eastwards overlooks pleasant if undramatic views of meadows and woodlands.

Of course, none of the villages in this part of Kent has any monopoly of the entrancing views, and Pluckley is another that boasts wide views of the distinctively Wealden countryside all around. It also claims—or has had claimed for it—that it is the most haunted village in England with at least a dozen ghost stories connected with the village during the last five hundred years. Quite a lot of the older houses in Pluckley were built by the Dering family, whose name lingers on in the fairly extensive Dering Wood, south-west of the village, in Surrenden Dering to the east, and Dering Farm south of the wood. Pluckley church contains a number of Dering family monuments and memorials, including the Dering chapel.

Southwards, still, and closing in on Ashford to the east, Great Chart is another attractive village of half-timbered houses as well as some quite modern ones. Singleton Manor, with its moat, is probably its most outstanding single building, not only for the fact that it was the home of Nicholas Toke who outlived five wives before, at the age of ninety-three, he set out to walk to London to find a sixth wife. He did not make it, but history thinks none the worse of him for that!

But we have reached Ashford too soon, hurrying westwards of villages like Westwell, just south-east of Charing and overlooking the river Stour. Although small, the village is notable both for its surrounding countryside, which is very beautiful, and for its age, which is considerable. The place was inhabited in Saxon times, and possibly long before that. It is on the trackway which has become known to us as the Pilgrim's Way, although it crossed southern England from east to west long before the pilgrimages to Canterbury began. The village was thrust into history's pages when Alexander Iden, who then lived at Ripple Court, found the fifteenth-century Kentish rebel Jack Cade hiding in his garden and took him into custody. Another Westwell notable was Richard Barham, author of the famous Ingoldsby Legends, who was curate here for part of his career.

All Saint's church at Boughton Aluph has an intriguing peculiarity in the rather fine fireplace in its south porch. The Canterbury pilgrims are said to have been in the habit of resting in the village —and perhaps of making use of the fireplace—until a large enough group of them had gathered to offer the safety of numbers along the way through Challock Forest, notorious for robbers in those days. Today's travellers can hope to catch a glimpse of the deer that roam the forest now.

Approaching Ashford from the north, the first warning of the town is the new development around the little village of Kennington, which uses the Ashford by-pass and the little Bybrook that trickles into the Great Stour on the other side of the road as physical frontiers between Kennington and Ashford.

A minor road from Kennington's Spearpoint Corner by-passes Ashford to meet up with the Folkestone road at Willesborough Lees, avoiding Hinxhill and the little village of Brook which snuggles against the Downs that rise above it on its north side, paddling its feet in the little waterway from which it takes its name.

This is one of the celebrated chalk streams for which south-east England is famous. Like most of them, this one has never been known to run dry. The village itself is not specially distinctive, except for its church which is reputedly one of the oldest in England. The tower is one of the largest of this early period in the country and nearby is a great medieval barn that now houses the Wye College museum of farm implements.

For ramblers, of course, Wye Downs are probably among the best bits of Kent, with spectacular views and charming little villages like Crundale and Hastingleigh. The Downs are a nature reserve and for naturalists who know what they are looking for there is a great variety of wildlife, including orchids and rare butterflies and moths, as well as many birds and insects.

Wye itself is rather more than a village—more a small country town. Whether it is best-known for its racecourse, or for its agricultural college (part of the University of London) or even for its parish church of SS Martin and Gregory probably depends upon to whom it is known. All three have claims to fame of different kinds, but perhaps, anyway, Wye is best known not for any of these so much as for the truly breathtaking beauty of the countryside in which it is set. Driving, riding or walking, this is East Kent at its superb best.

Hastingleigh is an attractive little village in the heart of the East Kent Downlands, overlooking the Stour Valley and a great base for ramblers and explorers of the countryside.

Nearby, Brabourne is another of those scattered villages apparently spilling down the southern slopes of the Downs. It is a three-part village: West Brabourne, East Brabourne and Brabourne Lees. Beautiful, though not specially interesting except for the East Brabourne church of St Mary, with its peculiarly massive tower, so squat that it does not actually tower at all.

The parish shares with the neighbouring parish of Smeeth the peculiarity of the boundary that divides the churchyard of the Baptist Church so that the church is in one parish and the porch in the other.

The Ashford by-pass emerges on to the A20 south-east of Ashford at Willesborough Lees, and continues eastwards past Willesborough Street and South Willesborough. South of the road and north of the Ashford–Folkestone railway line is Mersham, where Robert Adam built his first house of hand-made brick for Sir William Knatchbull. It became the manor house of Mersham-le-Hatch and belonged to the Knatchbull family from the first half of the sixteenth century. The present house was built during the ten years following 1762.

The road slices through the still-growing village of Sellindge and then, at the point where the A261 strikes off from the A20 towards Hythe, leaving the A20 itself to twitch almost at right angles in order to finish its journey to Folkestone, the old Roman

Stone Street, now the B2608, arrows northwards with no more than a single hiccup of a deviation from an otherwise dead straight ten or twelve miles into the heart of Canterbury without going directly through a single village all the way.

The parish of Stanford has its boundary proprietorially round the Folkestone (Dumpton Park) racecourse, close by the old fortified Westenhanger Manor House. In its prime, this massive building on a hill above Hythe had 126 rooms, 365 windows and a moat. Built in the fourteenth century on the site of a Saxon palace, it originally had nine towers, one of which is still standing today and is known as Fair Rosamund's tower in remembrance of the legend that Henry II's mistress, Rosamund Clifford, lived at the house. After the fifteenth-century improvements by Sir Edward Poyning, Lord-Deputy of Ireland, Elizabeth I visited the house and gave it to Sir Thomas Sackville. It played its part in the Civil War and was used as a prison for Royalists for a short time. Now, only three towers, the gatehouse and part of the courtyard remain and any real evidence that the Fair Rosamund did (as local tradition would very much like to insist she did) once live here is long lost.

Stone Street disdains villages like Postling although this is a truly charming little foot-of-the-Downs village, one of the show-pieces of which is the very fine half-timbered Tudor mansion known as Postling Court. A farm just outside the village was home to Joseph Conrad from 1899 until 1920, and he wrote some of his best novels during that period.

High above the village—597 feet high if we are being precise—is an ancient burial place on Tolsford Hill.

The only real deviation from its vertical north-south geometry on the map that Stone Street makes is at Monks Horton, no more than a hamlet, and a small one at that, but worth mention for the charm of its Tudor Kite Cottage, originally the local manor house. Nearby, are the remains of a twelfth-century Cluniac Priory which became a farmhouse after the Dissolution.

The road gives very little acknowledgement of the existence of

Stowting on its west side, but on Stowting Hill there is an ancient tumulus and just west of the village is the old Castle Mount. The church still bears witness to its Norman ancestry in the timbered porch, and the registers provide a written history back to 1539. The village actually takes its name from the river Stowe which passes Canterbury on its way to the sea near Sandwich.

At this point, the road passes through the south-western corner of Lyminge Forest, which hides little Rhodes Minnis from view, and heads in for Elmstead, a village of mixed woodland and open farm-land with a little Early English flint church that has an unusual tower steeple with a peal of six bells. Few places in Kent—or, indeed, anywhere else—can be said to be more truly rural than Elmsted.

Zig-zagging back to the eastern side of Stone Street again, still heading north, Stelling Minnis perches high over the run-down into Canterbury, an ideal site for the rather fine weather-boarded windmill which stands there, its two sails spread, mulling over the good old days before it was retired and became one of an ever-diminishing number of similar relics scattered about Kent.

'Minnis' is a word that has been variously defined but is gener-ally taken to mean common land or moorland and the village is, in fact, surrounded by moorland. Eastwards, towards Elham, Elham Park Wood and Clavertye Wood form two miles of very beautiful woodland country.

Back again to the west side of Stone Street, Waltham sits on a high spot for this part of the county, together with the associated hamlet of Anvil Green. Once known as Temple Waltham, it was then owned by the Knights Templar and its old brick and flint church has an intriguingly intricate oak beamed roof and a four-teenth-century triple sedilia in the chancel. Nearby Yockletts Bank is a nature reserve famous for its rare orchids.

The name of the once-illustrious Hadres family is perpetuated in the twin villages of Upper and Lower Hardres. The family owned this part of Kent for seven hundred years after the Norman Conquest, and it is said that Thomas Hardres, who was knighted for valour at the seige of Boulogne in 1544, brought back the gates of the French city and erected them at Upper Hardres.

Upper Hardres was an established settlement before the Normans arrived, though. The present church, thirteenth and fourteenth century for the most part, is on the site of a Saxon church. It boasts the only perfect brass of its bracket type in England; it depicts one John Strete (1405) in academic gown. The church also has some of the finest window glass in Kent.

All the villages along the line of Stone Street are particularly prettily sited; high above sea level, with views out over the distant countryside. Petham is another of them, with its nearby hamlet of Garlinge Green, where Iron Age Belgic cemetery relics have been recovered from Swarling Downs.

Nackington is a Canterbury suburb now, although it disguises the fact very well at the end of its cul-de-sac approach road leading into the small group of houses, farm buildings and church that are the old village.

Kicking off from the straight line of the old Roman road, the B2068 curves north-easterly past Lower Hardres to go through Nackington and emerge on to the A2, the main London–Dover Watling Street line, once the principal route for travellers between the country's capital and the chief of the Channel Ports. Today the A20 is a strong rival for that role, and the A2 is cursed and vilified by residents of the villages through which it passes because of the enormous volume of very heavy inter-Continental traffic it brings through them.

One of the most vociferous of these—with good reason—has been the village of Bridge, an attractive enough little group of brick and weather-board buildings, where the full weight, noise and danger of modern traffic is still being taken by an eighteenth-century brick bridge over the Little Stour, also known as the Nail Bourne. The village is at the bottom of a hill from whichever direction the A2 enters it, and it cannot be denied that the speed restriction signs at either end are not as effective as they might be. Villagers have pressed for a by-pass to take the traffic round the village and enable the little church with its Norman doorways and its stone figure of Macobus Kasey (1512) in his priest's robes, to go back to sleep again, unafraid of the damaging effects of vibration and exhaust fumes. The go-ahead has been given for the building of the new road, but the wheels of the administrative machinery grind vastly more slowly than do the wheels of commerce, and who can blame the good people of Bridge, and other villages like it, if they become impatient?

Both Patrixbourne and Bekesbourne have fared better than Bridge, since the A2 passes south of both of them. Patrixbourne is a very old settlement indeed. Early British, Roman, Danish and Saxon settlers have all left their imprint within the parish, and it is generally accepted that this is the site of the battle in which Caesar defeated the Britons in his successful second invasion.

Most of the older houses in the village today do not pre-date the mid-nineteenth century, although they look older with their half-timbering and thatch, and the Nail Bourne in whose valley the village sits waters the road from time to time in a picturesque, if locally inconvenient, manner.

But the church remains as a reminder of the genuine antiquity of the place. Built about 1160, its Norman tower carries a thirteenth-century shingled spire and the south doorway is a particularly fine one for its age, rich in intricate sculpture and ornamentation. Bifrons, once a Stuart manor house and country seat of the Marquis of Conyngham, was demolished in 1950, but although gone it is not forgotten. There remains the Bifrons chapel in the church, with its Swiss glass dating from 1538 and 1670.

Nearby Bekesbourne was once a borough in it own right and a member of the Cinque Port of Hastings. Bekesbourne Place, once owned by Archbishop Cranmer who stayed there before his imprisonment and martydrom, was built during Tudor times but altered considerably in the eighteenth century. Now, more than the village itself, it is Howletts, home of Mr John Aspinall's private zoo, just outside the village, that attracts much of the attention in these parts.

Further east the wooded hills around Adisham were familiar to travellers in prehistoric times. Their track became today's Pilgrims' Way and there was a church in Adisham as early as A.D. 616. The present one, however, was built in the thirteenth century, and there is a tomb slab that commemorates Thomas Upton, rector until he died in 1310, and a very large bronze statue of Thomas à Becket outside the west door. There is also some rather fine woodwork with paintings, originally made seven hundred years ago for Canterbury Cathedral.

On the south side of the A2, amid the wooded slopes rising up from the Little Stour valley, Bishopsbourne's most distinctive feature is certainly Bourne House, one of the finest Queen Anne houses in Kent. But the village also boasts a rectory that seems to inspire literary distinction in its residents. It was here that Richard Hooker (rector from 1595 until 1600) completed his "The Laws of Ecclesiastical Polity", which contributed significantly to moderating the views of the English church at that time. Later, the rectory was the home of Joseph Conrad, the Polish exile who found fame—and some fortune—as a fiction writer in Kent.

At this point, the B2065 leaves the A2 and winds its own way southwards towards Folkestone and Hythe, through Kingston and across the beautiful Barham Downs.

Here is another part of Kent that has yielded up evidence of occupation by prehistoric man, Romans, Danes and Saxons in their turn.

Barham windmill was once a notable East Kent landmark and was scheduled for preservation by Kent County Council. It passed into the county council's ownership in 1967 but the whole super-structure was destroyed by fire during restoration in 1970. The council did toy with the idea of leaving the stubby base and allow-ing the surrounding land to be used as a designated picnic site, but the area was small and it was finally decided to sell the land and forget all about the vanished landmark.

Just south of Barham, where the A260 strikes off from the A2 to go to Folkestone, is the very beautiful expanse of Broome Park, a seventeenth-century country house, now a hotel, but once owned by Lord Kitchener who, however, never lived in it.

Nearby hamlets include Derringstone and Breach, and then the road goes on through Wingmore and Elham, treating its travellers to one of the scenic delights of the county, the Elham Valley.

Elham village is almost too big to be so called. It is almost a little town, with a High Street flanked by houses of very different periods and styles, from the half-timbered houses with upper storeys supported by carved brackets and the fifteenth-century inn, now the Abbotts Fireside Hotel, the brick-red houses around the little Market Square, and the more modern appearance of the villas at either end. The grey stone church is an imposing building with a battlemented tower and a steeple for a peal of eight bells. The vestry still contains many of the eight hundred books given by Mr Lee Warley for the use of the parishioners in 1809, although about three hundred volumes are now lodged in the Hawley-Harrison Library at Canterbury Cathedral where, under the terms of the bequest, they can be seen by any Elham parishioner who asks for them.

But Elham has not outgrown village status on its way towards becoming a small town. Quite the reverse, in fact, for it was once a market town with a Charter granted by Prince Edward (before he became Edward I) that allowed the townsfolk to hold a market there every Monday. Some of the buildings at the Market Square end of the village may even remember the colourful bustle of those long-ago Mondays at Elham.

Just east of the road is Acrise, a scattered village entrenched among winding country lanes through woodlands, where the church stands actually in the grounds of Acrise Place, a red-brick mansion built during the reign of Henry VII. The church is of Norman origins and well endowed with reminders of the Papillon family that for so long owned Acrise Place.

Another 'almost a town' village is Lyminge, where today's

Early English church has built into it some of the fabric of the earlier Saxon church, and stands on the site of a church which may have been built here before the Christian era was five hundred years old. It was here that St Ethelburga of Northumbria founded a nunnery, and was buried in 647. Lyminge became the Christian centre of England during her lifetime. Very little remains today of that nunnery, but there is a bridle track known locally as Ethelburga's Grove, and the present church is dedicated to SS Mary and Ethelburga.

Also vanished, this time quite without trace, is the old manor house where the Archibshops of Canterbury lived during the twelfth and thirteenth centuries. But there does remain a fine modern Methodist Church, impressive in its simple dignity, and a lovely Queen Anne house, Sibton Hall, which is now a girls' preparatory school standing in its own sixty-eight-acre park.

Etchinghill is a hamlet in the parish of Lyminge; a pretty place, the principal building in which is St Mary's Hospital.

Now we are back on the A20, just outside Newington where Thomas à Becket stayed in 1170 on his return from Rome. There are several seventeenth- and eighteenth-century houses in Newington, and at nearby Frogholt there is a very old, timber-framed Kent Cottage, which is an ancient monument. The gardens at Frogholt House at Newington are open to the public during the summer.

Both Newington and Frogholt are threatened with encirclement by new roads into the proposed Cheriton terminal for the Channel tunnel. Some authorities forecast that the effect will be serious enough to make it necessary for the Government to buy out both villages rather than to ask residents to live among the new environment. If that happens, two attractive little villages may have to die sacrificially in order that the tunnel shall be born, and there is no lack of voices to condemn such an exchange. Yet, if it happens, no doubt within a lifetime—probably much less—no-one will even remember that either Newington or Frogholt, and possibly some other settlements in the vicinity, were once where the new tunnel-born development are their only monuments.

Right on the outskirts of Hythe is the very attractive little village of Saltwood, with a timbered village hall and a pleasant little village green. There was some sort of castle here at the time of Domesday and the village earned its name from the use of the local wood to boil off the sea-water taken from the salt pans along the seashore.

Today's Saltwood Castle is a massive stone fortification, the restored remains of that castle where Thomas à Becket's murderers met before setting out on their historic mission to Canterbury. Since then, it has been the residence of Lords Warden of the Cinque Ports, the home of the Deedes family, and after it fell into ruins about a hundred years ago, it was bought and restored by the late Lady Ira Conway, and is now the home of historian Lord Clark and Lady Clark.

We are now back on the verge of Romney Marsh again, but a turn northwards leads to Paddlesworth, well and truly above sea level and the Marsh. The little nine hundred years old church of St Oswald at Paddlesworth is one of many contenders for inclusion in that select group of 'smallest churches in Britain'. At the last census in 1971, Paddlesworth parish achieved the distinction of having fewest inhabitants of all the inhabited parishes in Kent. The figure given was 35 people—18 male and 17 female in 10 households.

The coastal village of Capel le Ferne tries hard to reach out and hold hands with neighbouring Folkestone and it will surely succeed before too long. Already the village is a large one, almost wholly residential in character, astride the main Folkestone to Dover A20 road. The 2,000 residents are joined every summer by many campers who use the nearby camping site and caravan parks both as holiday homes and as staging-posts before embarking for Continental destinations at the Channel ports, or for somewhere to rest and recover from the effects of the crossing before going on to inland Britain destinations.

West Hougham (say *Huffem*) is just north of the A20 and very different from its nearest neighbour, Capel le Ferne. For one thing it is almost wholly agricultural, and it gave its name to Robert de Hougham, a Crusader who fought with the King at the Siege of St John d'Acre in the Holy Lane and who returned to find his local church in urgent need of restoration. He celebrated his homecoming by having the work done and the church stands testimony to the benevolence of the local crusader to this day.

Just east of Paddlesworth and on the busy main A260 road that links Folkestone with the A2, Hawkinge has sprawled a good deal in the comparatively recent past, in the wake of the growth of Folkestone itself.

Hawkinge used to have an airfield, and was in fact one of the first RAF stations. The airfield is still there, literally, although it is no longer used and has become one with the rest of the village history, like the old White Horse Inn, Flegis Court and other remnants of a long antiquity.

Between Hawkinge and River, Alkham seems to have snuggled itself down into a fold of the hills and drawn a quilt of trees round its ears. The B2060 passes through the village, which is clustered round the cross-roads thus formed by minor roads leading off to the north-west and the south-east. Part of Sandgate Castle was built of stone which Henry VIII had removed from St Radegund's Abbey which was once near Alkham.

Through Densole, the road goes on to Swingfield, high above Folkestone, where the Knights Hospitallers have left their preceptory in the form of St John's Farm, now owned by Kent County Council and all set for restoration before being opened to the public.

By-passing Wootton, the road goes through Denton to rejoin the A2. Denton is just what a rural village ought to be: a village green overlooked by half-timbered and tiled cottages and always managing to look as though it has just cleaned itself up. Beside the church, the eighteenth-century Denton Court stands in about two hundred acres of ground. It was once the home of Sir Egerton

Brydges, author of the ten volumes of *Titles and Opinions of Old English Books*. The house was rebuilt in 1860 after it was damaged by a serious fire. It was also a favourite lodging-place of the poet Gray.

Richard Barham's *Ingoldsby Legends* reached out into this part of Kent for their subject-matter, and the author's family home was at Tappington Farm, which is featured in the *Legends*.

Wootton is smaller than Denton, but hardly less attractive in its wooded countryside, but Lydden, nestling at the foot of the Downs in the valley through which the road and the railway run on the way to Dover, is quite large, with a pond overlooked by some rather fine trees. Just outside the village, to the north-west, is the Lydden circuit, a well-known track where there are regular meetings for car and motor-cycle racing.

Practically part of Dover now, the twin villages of Temple Ewell and River, straddle the junction of the A256 Sandwich road with the A2. River, in fact, is now almost wholly within the Dover urban area, the two communities having reached out to tag each other as the good road and rail services have attracted residential infilling between them.

Nevertheless, some relics of former times remain, including the old River water mill which was restored at a cost of £30,000 and then presented to Dover Corporation for a peppercorn rent by a St Mary's Bay property owner. The village is set on the wooded slopes of Temple Ewell Downs, which are protected for the special scientific interest of the wildlife and which swoop down upon the port of Dover itself.

Temple Ewell, with its own small shopping centre, takes its name from the Knights Templar, who had one of their preceptories here. It was here, too, that King John met Poundulf, representative of the Pope, in 1213 before he went down into Dover to surrender to the Pope's demands. After the Knights Templar were suppressed, the manor passed to the Knights Hospitallers.

Nearby Kearsney Abbey is quite modern. It is owned by Dover Corporation as a public park, a feature of which is the lake formed

by the Dour which flows on through the town of Dover into the
sea. There is also an open-air theatre in the park. Opposite the
Abbey, are Russell Gardens, celebrated for their lake and water-
falls, a very pleasant memorial to a former rural district councillor.

The A256 heads north to Sandwich, forming the base of a
triangle, the other two sides of which are the A2 and the A257.
Inside the triangle are some fine, high woodlands and farmlands,
sprinkled with villages, many of which are as attractive as any in
the county.

Villages like Coldred and Shepherdswell, once independent
parishes, but since 1936 sharing the same parish boundaries.
The London–Dover railway line cuts through the hills under the
village by way of the Shepherdswell tunnel, but this was well
settled countryside long before the Industrial Revolution gave
birth to the railways.

Shepherdswell is still sometimes referred to by its older name
of Sibertswold and both Roman and Saxon remains have been dug
up in the parish. Three Barrow Down is the site of much older
tumuli.

So it has long been a residential site, and today its proximity to
the Kent coalfield and to the port of Dover, coupled with its railway station and conveniently close main road links with Canterbury and the coast, all combine to make this a still growing community. However, in spite of all the new homes that have been
added to the older core, the village still centres on the pretty
little village green with its fence of stately chestnut trees, the
village inn, the school, and the church.

Coldred, which is smaller and rather more truly rural, is another
settlement with its roots in a Roman past. The church, dedicated
to St Pancras, is built on the site of a Roman camp, and is largely
Saxon in origin. It claims that its one broken bell is one of the
oldest in Britain—and as far as I know, no-one has ever disputed
it. The very name of the village is a clear echo of the name of that

Typical Wealden weatherboard architecture at Hawkhurst


Old houses and the church, Goudhurst

Famous Weald of Kent landmark: Cranbrook Mill

One of the finest moated houses in England, thirteenth-century
Ightham Mote

The Watersplash at Eynsford

The gateway, Lullingstone Castle

King of Mercia, Ceoldred, who fought the Saxons on this spot in 715.

Nearby Waldershare Park, seat of the Earl of Guilford, are five hundred acres of beautiful beech trees, limes and chestnuts. The manor was once the property of Bishop Odo, brother of William the Conqueror, who possessed himself of a very great deal of some of the best Kentish property after the Conquest.

North again is another mining village, Eythorne, and the well-wooded surrounds of Barfrestone which, although very small, attracts thousands of visitors every year to see its uniquely beautiful and lavishly carved little Norman church.

To the west, past Woollage Green, is Womenswould, in the angle formed by the junction of the B2406 with the Watling Street A2. Woollage Green is heavily wooded, and Womenswould itself is another of the Kent colliery villages although it has none of the rather harsh utilitarianism of neighbouring Aylesham and is, in fact, more truly 'villagy' than some of the more obviously agriculture-based rural villages of East Kent.

Aylesham is almost wholly modern; a 'new village' founded in the 1920s as the home of Snowdown Colliery workers nearly fifty years ago. Today it has a population of more than 4,000 people, and an industrial estate established by the old Eastry rural council as a means of diversifying local employment opportunities and to relieve the dependence of the local community on coal.

Back alongside the Sandwich road is Tilmanstone, still fast in the Kent coalfield, and much modernized and filled out with new building. But, like other villages hereabouts, Tilmanstone is no johnny-come-lately, if the local belief that the churchyard yew tree is 1,000 years old is true.

An attractive village, approached from the east, of thatch and tile, is Nonington, whose main street wriggles ecstatically between the mainly old houses—including historic thirteenth-century Southdown Cottage—as though trying to delay emerging almost at the very gate of Snowdown Colliery at the western end.

Nearer the centre of the triangle formed by the main roads,

G

is Chillenden, not to be missed because of the hundred-year-old Chillenden windmill, white-painted and standing in the middle of a field on a local high spot (170 feet above sea level) of the long slow slope up from the Sandwich coastline towards Barham Downs.

It is not easy, today, to imagine that the little village of Eastry was once capital of the seven lathes into which the Kingdom of Kent was divided. But it has been important for many, many years, and hard by the church is the Georgian façade of Eastry Court, which today marks the site of the one-time royal hall of Kentish Kings. Lord Nelson and Lady Hamilton used to come to Heronden House at Eastry and no doubt knew well, even if only from the outside, the 'Bull Inn' and the 'Five Bells' in the village.

Did they also know about the extensive arched caverns and caves under the garden of Beckets in Woodnesborough Lane? Experts are divided about whether they are as much as 4,000 years old, or much more modern. Certainly, at nearby Hammill brick-works a 70 foot claypit shaft yielded up a Romano-Belgic type jar thought to have been about 2,000 years old.

Goodnestone keeps its old character by the simple ruse of presenting a 'No through road' sign to anyone who stumbles upon the approach to its village street. But the incurably inquisitive— and those with less idle reason for following the road to its dead end—will find a quaint little place, with its school and its church and its pub, the 'Fitzwalter Arms' all looking very much of a single unit that makes no pretence at a welcome for strangers.

At the crossroads that must have witnessed many an idly curious traveller's indecision about whether to fork right into Sandwich or left into Ash, is Woodnesborough, the name of which goes right back to the pagan Norse god, Woden. Legend alone now supports the contention that Firtree Hill outside the village was a place where pre-Christian residents held their local prayer-meetings and nearby Beacon Hill recalls the days when the Wantsum was still a shipping channel in need of guiding lights from surrounding prominences.

Much later in the history of the district, Flemish refugees who came to Sandwich spread out into the surrounding countryside and left their distinctive architectural style in villages like Woodnesborough.

Nearby Staple, which hangs pendant-like between Ash and Wingham, has comparatively little of interest outside the church. Even the moat that once surrounded the Tudor Crixhall Court is gone now. But on the very outskirts of the village, going towards Aylesham, Reed Cottage is worth a second look if only for the thatched roof that is a vanishing feature of the Kentish countryside these days.

Across the A257 Canterbury–Sandwich Road from Wingham is a little group of villages, the nearest of which is Ickham, in the parish of Ickham and Well which also includes the hamlets of Bramling, Seaton and Upper Garrington.

Ickham is a village of attractive cottages along the street on either side of the village green and the church. Most of the houses are old—one, well preserved still, dates from 1200; and there are records to prove that Offa, King of Mercia, gave land in the parish to Christ Church, Canterbury, in 791.

Another of the group of villages is Littlebourne, upstream on the Little Stour of Wickhambreaux, with a mill of its own among the river's crowding willows. This is hop-growing country, of course, and Littlebourne is beset by oast houses and a tithe barn. The High Street is comfortingly enclosed at one end by the unusually named Evenhill Inn, and at the other by 'The Anchor'.

Nearby Bramling is a small cluster of houses alongside the A2, with one particularly eyecatching building no passer-by could possibly overlook, the very handsome red brick house that is now Bramling House hotel.

This tour of the villages of East Kent has so far left out those coastal villages seawards of the A256 between Sandwich and Dover.

Immediately south of Sandwich is Worth, where the shingled

spire of the church reaches above the surrounding trees to peer through slatted bell tower louvres at The Street and south again Ham is yet another of those villages that likes to lay claim to one of the smallest churches in Kent. Ham is fairly unusual among Kent villages, too, for the number of thatched cottages it retains.

But continuing south in Sholden we run into the almost inevitable modern development that has done its best to bridge the countryside gap between the village and the town and port of Deal.

Further inland, Northbourne has managed to hang on to its antique charms in spite of a fair amount of modernity here and there, and in spite, too, of having Kent's largest colliery, Betteshanger, little more than a stone's throw away across the fields, behind the church. In the grounds of Northbourne Court, home of Lord Northbourne, two small skeletons were found within the walls of the remains of an ancient abbey. Locally, they will tell you that the bones were those of two young princes who were murdered at nearby Eastry in the mid-seventh century.

Betteshanger is a very attractive parkland and farmland estate belonging to Lord Northbourne, which, if it needs to claim fame, can always fall back on the churchyard yew tree planted by Gladstone.

Past Great and Little Mongeham, the church at Ripple is as modern as about a hundred years old, although it is on the site of a thirteenth-century church. But it, too, has its point of pride in the simple grave of Field Marshal Sir John French, Earl Ypres. One of the two yew trees in the churchyard was there when the Domesday Survey was made.

Sutton's church has a less distinguished paragraph in history. Part of it fell down during the earth tremor in 1580.

There are four centres of population in the parish of Langdon: East and West Langdon, Martin and Martin Mill. Close to West Langdon are what remains of Langdon Abbey, founded in 1189 and a victim of the Dissolution, but honoured with a reputed visit from King Edward II in 1325. There is still a Langdon Abbey today, but it is a large red-brick house of distinctly lay design and whatever remains of the old abbey is below ground level. East Langdon has an attractive village green, but both Martin and Martin Mill are resort-style villages in fairly modern idiom.

Quite how Ringwould has managed to stay so rural-looking right on the edge of Deal and across the main Dover–Deal road is something of a wonder. There are old cottages and some Bronze Age barrows and the odd little cupola on top of the church tower's corner turret is a landmark for sea and land travellers alike.

Part of Ringwould parish, but quite distinct as a village, is Kingsdown, a coastal resort and really now a continuation of the Walmer seafront. But the village deserves its separate consideration if only for the fact that it was here that Julius Caesar first set foot on English soil in 55 B.C. Caesar would not recognize the place today, but there are a number of old cottages among the predominantly modern development, which includes a small, modern shopping centre.

Hard by Dover's town boundaries, Whitfield is almost completely built-up, with new housing estates and shopping centres. But history—or, at any rate, legend—dies hard in these parts and Archers Court Secondary School at Whitfield commemorates the Knight of Archers Court manor, whose terms of tenure required him to accompany the monarch whenever he crossed the English Channel and hold a silver bowl for the King, should the sovereign of the day not be a particularly good sailor. Much more recently, Whitfield had one of the first aerodromes in England, and it was here that the first cross-Channel competitive flight ended in 1910.

St Margaret's at Cliffe cranes over the cliff top above the seaside resort of St Margaret's Bay. The village has every modern convenience for the large and still growing holiday camp and caravan community, including a praticularly fine and almost unaltered Norman church which, in spite of a hit from a cross-Channel shell during the Second World War is still well worth a place on any local holidaymaker's itinerary of sights to see.

St Margaret's Bay is not a village in any conventional sense of the word, although the resident population might permit its inclusion under that heading. It is a place of hotels and guest houses and, above all, of parking spaces most of which overlook the sea and the bay. A landmark on the top of the cliffs is the Dover Patrol obelisk, built in 1921. It is one of a 'set', the others being at Cap Blanc Nez in France and in New York Harbour. The monument is a 90 foot high stone column designed by Sir Aston Webb commemorating the Royal Navy's First World War Channel patrols.

From 'Goose Fair' to 'Guston' sounds an unlikely enough corruption, but it is said that Guston got its name from the goose fair that was once a local feature. Two miles out of Dover, behind the castle, Guston is best-known (particularly, perhaps, to air travellers) for the shape of an aeroplane planted in granite into the cliff-top turf, a reminder that this was the spot where Louis Bleriot landed the first cross-Channel aeroplane on 25th July 1909.

It is to Guston, too, that visitors to Dover come to stand on the cliffs and look down, as though at some wonderfully detailed working model spread below them, at the bustling business of Dover's Eastern Docks, with the cross-Channel ferry berths and the hovercraft gorging and disgorging their interminable cargoes of cars and people.

5

# The Weald

I T is probably true to say that most people, invited to illustrate a typical Kentish scene, would draw a hop garden, probably with an orchard alongside, and certainly an oast house with one or more round kilns, each with a white wooden cowl on top, and perhaps a metal rampant horse on each vane. Yet, in fact, that picture is not typical of most of Kent at all, but only of one, fairly large and even more important, area: the Weald. And not even all of the Weald, which is not one area but at least two: the low Weald, which is really mid-Kent around Maidstone, particularly to the south of Maidstone; and the high Weald, which spills over the southern boundary of the county into East Sussex. For all that the two are usually spoken of as though they were one, they are, in fact, two quite different regions.

The High Weald is heavily wooded, still very similar in character in many places to that Weald which was known to very early settlers as Andresweald—the Forest of Andres. This is the county's cattle country, its Far West, and there is a strong element of the Wild West in its history, too. It was the Andresweald that kept Sussex a pagan place for so long after Kent was Christianized. The forest was almost impenetrable when Augustine brought the new faith to Thanet, and although the Romans built one of their incredible roads right through the Weald, very few traces of it have been discovered since.

Early farmers tended to confine their labours to the most hospitable soils, like those of the North Kent coastal strip, Thanet, and the river valleys. Up in the High Weald, the soil is almost everywhere unpredictable (with several different soils in one field, often enough), heavy and generally difficult to farm. That is why, even today, the greater part of the High Weald is given over to pasture land and woods. At the time of the Norman Conquest, there were no more than a few frontiersmen subsisting in their forest clearings (the 'dens' that have left us the characteristic place-names throughout the whole of the Weald—places like Marden, Tenterden, Frittenden, Horsmonden, Benenden, and so on)—all of them attached in the feudal system to one or other of the older and larger settlements in the north.

It was not until the eighth century that men began to move into the Weald at all and when the Domesday Survey was made the whole of the area right along the county's southern boundary was almost completely unoccupied. Certainly, there were virtually no manors in the Weald.

Succeeding centuries brought changes only slowly to this lovely but somewhat inhospitable region. By Tudor times, though, it was the Black Country of southern England, its dens ringing with the clamour of the iron industry that grew and flourished here. In the second half of the sixteenth century, there were eight furnaces in the Kentish Weald, using what must then have seemed like an inexhaustable supply of timber fuel for the furnaces of the foundries that manufactured iron cannons and cannon balls and domestic ironware, as well. Practically all that remains of this once vast industry are the hammer ponds, many of them completely camouflaged in undergrowth and coppice but a few, in recent years, restored to at least some usefulness by being cleared and stocked with fish and made into very attractive resorts for anglers fortunate enough to be friends with the farmers on whose land the ponds lie.

Then, came the woollen industry, which, for a time, buoyed up the Wealdon economy, using local and particularly the neighbouring Romney Marsh fleeces and the essential fullers' earth which is still quarried outside Maidstone to produce some of Britain's finest cloths.

But then the great coal mines of the Midlands and the North of England gradually opened up and steam replaced water and man-power as the main source of industrial energy and the Weald was left to earn recognition from today's Countryside Commission as one of the five highest priority areas of outstanding natural beauty in the whole country. The accolade was specially welcomed by those enthusiasts who formed in 1960 and who perpetuate today the Weald of Kent Preservation Society which has done and still does such good work on behalf of the area it is concerned with, both in collaboration with but, when necessary, also in opposition to, local authorities and the planners.

For centuries, Tenterden—which is on the rim of the Romney Marsh, geographically—was regarded as the capital of the Weald, and is, indeed, still so described by many writers today. Certainly, it began as did so many Wealden villages, as a manorial outpost, a 'den' of the people of Thanet. But it very early achieved inde-pendent status as a borough and a limb of the Cinque Port of Rye.

But it was Cranbrook that gave its name to the rural district that covered most of the southern Weald until the 1974 local govern-ment reorganization, and there is no doubt that the village is, in some ways, more typically Wealden in its close-huddled weather-boarding than the much more expansive town of Tenterden.

Let us set out from Tenterden and take the high road (well, to be more specific, the A28) northwards as though en route for Ash-ford. That brings us first to High Halden, overlooking the Beult valley. The river Beult is a tributary of the river Medway, and rises in the Wealden Ridge a mile or two south-east of High Halden village. Progress has overtaken the village to some extent; in 1828 Ireland dismissed it as "unpleasant as any in the county", which was a bit harsh, although truth to tell, there is something uncompromisingly unlovely about High Halden itself. Once a haunt of smugglers, including the notorious Ransley family who were the

Jesse James' of Kent's Wild West a hundred years before the American West was terrorized by that gang, High Halden enjoyed a quieter reputation for the characteristic brown and yellow High Halden pottery which was produced near today's Potkiln Farm.

About mid-way between Tenterden and Ashford is the village of Bethersden, which has given its name to the Bethersden marble that used to be quarried nearby. It was not marble, really, but a stone veined with fossilized shell. There is a highly polished piece of Bethersden marble in Rochester Cathedral and the altar stairs at Canterbury Cathedral are of Bethersden marble, too. Pieces have been incorporated into church towers, like those at Smarden and Tenterden, and it crops up in flooring, memorial slabs and fonts, as well as street paving (as at Biddenden) and field causeways formerly used by pack horses. The Bethersden marble is no longer quarried. What remains today is too soft to be of any great value and is left where it is. Bethersden is absolutely typical of its region, with weatherboarded houses and a big Perpendicular period church, and proudly recalls that in 1972 it was winner of the East Kent large villages section of the Kent's Best Kept Villages competition.

Smarden is particularly fortunate in its number of old and picturesque houses, several of which date from Tudor times, like Chessenden House which was built during the reign of Elizabeth I. It was Elizabeth, too, who signed the Charter that confirmed a much earlier one granted by Edward III in 1332 which gave Smarden the valuable right to hold a weekly market and an annual fair in the village.

The fourteenth-century village church of St Michael is sometimes referred to as 'The Barn of Kent' because of the unusually massive span of its roof. I suppose it is a bit barn-like from some angles but not, I think, disproportionately. Its castellated square tower, strongly buttressed, soars above the surrounding trees and provides a distinctive landmark. There is a story about a former Rector of Smarden who fell into a local bog and called to a ploughman working in a nearby field to save him. Rather than spoil his furrow by stopping midway, the ploughman said he would help, but added: "There's no hurry! Parson won't be needed 'til Sunday." There are probably half a hundred other villages all over England of which the same story is told—which does nothing to spoil it when told about Smarden.

A case could be made for a claim by Biddenden to be Kent's best-known village. Architecturally, it is both interesting and picturesque, with its timbered and tiled houses and shops, and its wide High Street which has not yet begun to feel the full crushing weight of modern heavy traffic that has so severely damaged so many contenders for the title of Kent's most picturesque villages.

The appearance of the village would have been quite enough to have ensured its fame in the twentieth century. But, in fact, the village fame rests most securely upon the two twelfth-century residents, Eliza and Mary Chulkhurst, Siamese twins joined at the shoulders and hips, who lived and took an active part in village life for thirty-four years. To this day, every Easter, the sisters are remembered by their bequest of a distribution of bread and cheese to the local poor. Today, special biscuits are baked with a representation of the twins stamped on them, and these are given to visitors to the bread and cheese ceremony.

But even the sisters did not exhaust the distinctions that time has loaded upon this so typical Wealden village. Biddenden was important as a centre of the Weald's cloth-making industry and along the north side of the High Street, between the little triangular green and the church, there is still a row of red-brick houses under one tiled roof below which, in one single long attic, the cloth workers of old earned their daily bread. Sadly, outside the High Street area, there has been some rather unsympathetic new building—there is too much of it and it does not fit in particularly well with the older traditions of the village centre. It is always a pity when this sort of thing happens, but nowhere more so than in a village endowed with the natural charms of Biddenden. In the last few years, the village has made a new bid for fame by joining the Kentish wine growing districts; a commercial vineyard has been established and already has a growing reputation at Little Whatmans.

At the edge of Biddenden parish lies the little hamlet of Three Chimneys, around the inn of the same name, at a point where three roads meet. The inn sign shows a soldier looking up at a three-finger sign post and the tale is told of French soldiers imprisoned at Sissinghurst Castle in the mid-eighteenth century referring to the junction as *les trois chemins* (the three roads), which was locally interpreted as Three Chimneys. It is a rather colourful little legend, but like many another legend, is unsupported by research which reveals that the Three Chimneys name for the junction pre-dates any French prisoners of war by a least two hundred years.

South of Tenterden, the first encounter is with the village of Rolvenden; a large village perched high on the Wealden Ridge among woodlands that probably did not look very different five or six—perhaps more—centuries ago. It is an attractive village, too, its curving High Street flanked by the weather-boarded buildings that typify Wealden architectural styles. In fact, the village is almost wholly post-seventeenth century, because it was burned down then, and the refugees moved out and down the hill into Rolvenden Layne. Incidentally, if the 'y' in Layne is puzzling, it is only because the Rolvenden dialect is unfamiliar. Listen to a local native's pronunciation of the word; certainly there is a 'y' in it!

John Wesley preached from Wesley House in Rolvenden Layne in 1758, and Great Maytham Hall, designed by Lutyens as a great mansion house, has been converted into private homes now, but is still open to visitors during the summer.

North of Rolvenden is Halden Place, where Lady Jane Grey once lived. Halden Park was, in King Edward V's day, the largest park in all England. And westward out of Rolvenden, towards Benenden, the road by-passes Rolvenden Mill, a particularly fine example of a post-mill, which has been restored.

A real frontier village is Newenden, closer to the Sussex border on the Kent side than any other village in Kent. Although Newenden might be said to be little more than a hamlet today, it was once a place of some importance, at the end of the wide Rother estuary, and its siting made it strategically important as a stronghold against invasion threats to the Weald from the sea across the Rother Levels, the Sussex equivalent of the Romney Marsh flatlands. But, as the river silted up, Newenden became more and more deeply landlocked, and less and less important. No doubt this loss of status has contributed to rather than detracted from its charm. It is not a pretty village in the company of many of the Wealden villages, but there is a remote charm about it that is enhanced by some very attractive old houses, and the church is interesting if only for its rather odd sawn-off look. In 1700 the chancel and tower of the old church were pulled down and today the church has an unusual little steeple on its disproportionately tiny tower. But it has kept its specially finely ornamented font carved with a set of Saxon dragons. Incidentally, it is claimed for Newenden that here the first recorded game of cricket was played during the reign of Edward I, but it is a claim that it might have difficulty in substantiating to the satisfaction of some authorities.

The road between Newenden and Hawkhurst runs along a ridge and through the village of Sandhurst, with its Upper and Lower Greens that were once one, and a somewhat incongruous and not remarkably beautiful clock tower.

The village architecture ranges very widely through the centuries up to the present time, for like most villages hereabouts, Sandhurst is still growing. In the fourteenth century, the Black Death threatened to wipe out Sandhurst, as it wiped out other villages all over England. But in fact, survivors buried their dead in the little churchyard and moved out, northwards—not very far, but far enough to call for some explanation of why the church seems to stand so far aloof from the main centre of occupation today. The church has an exceptionally massive fourteenth-century tower from which, it is claimed, the French coast can be seen on that fabulous 'fine day'. Just outside the village, south of the church, is Old Place farmhouse, recalling the original Court Lodge of Sandhurst.

Hawkhurst is a large village at the point where five roads star outwards: south for Hastings (A229); west to Hurst Green and on into deepest Sussex (A265); north-west to Lamberhurst and Tonbridge (A268); north to Cranbrook; and east back along the A268 to Sandhurst and Newenden before crossing into Sussex and heading for Rye.

The place-name suffix 'hurst' derives from the Saxon word for a wood and is usually prefixed by a derivation of a personal name. Not surprisingly, therefore, there are almost as many 'hursts' as 'dens' in the Weald, and Hawkhurst is one of them. Today, it has many of the characteristics of a small country town rather than a village. Once, it was an important centre of the Weald's iron industries, and it was also a centre of the Wealden cloth industry. Both those industries declined and died, but Hawkhurst was fortunate enough to be able to salvage its fallen fortunes with the help of the comparatively new hop-growing agriculture and that, in its turn, became one of the mainstays of the local economy. Now, hop-growing is declining, and although there are as yet no signs that it might die out altogether, it is certainly not quite as important a Kentish crop as it was even twenty years ago.

Hawkhurst today is a largely residential village of great charm, though, especially where the old and typically Wealden weather-boarded houses face the tree-lined Moor which, with the large, golden-brown sandstone church, forms the focal point of the old village. The newer shopping centre is at Highgate, where the roads join, which is chiefly remarkable for its Regency colonnade of shops.

Have you ever heard of Hemsted? Probably not, unless you already live nearby. Even then, you might not know that one of Sir Joshua Reynolds' favourite models, the eighteenth-century beauty Kitty Fisher, was the wife of one of the owners of the house. Actually, Hemsted was a manor long before William the

Conqueror arrived and began to redistribute all the best bits of England among his supporters 'for services rendered', and the house was built and altered several times before the present Victorian mansion (built in Jacobean style, just to confuse the unwary) came into the ownership of Viscount Rothermere. A more recent distinguished resident at Hemsted was Princess Anne, for the house is now the world-famous girls' public school known simply as Benenden, and is probably more widely known than the village from which it takes its name ever was.

Civil Servants know about Benenden because of its chest hospital; and horse riders know about Moat House riding school, where Princess Anne was a regular pupil. But the village itself is, after all, quite small: a few shops, a few houses, and planning restrictions have been exercised fairly rigorously to make sure it stays that way. A little aside from the village proper is a public house called 'Castleton's Oak' which has for a sign a picture of an old man sitting on a coffin. There is—naturally!—a story to go with such a curiously macabre sign, which tells how a certain Ebenezer Castleton made his own coffin when he was 70 years old, and had to live with it for another thirty years before he finally needed it.

Bendenden Green was given to the parish in 1928 by Lord Cranbrook and several to-be-great cricketers learned their skills on the pitch there. The village recreation field, where the annual fair is now held, was given to the parish by Lord Rothermere.

The Forestry Commission has plans to make a picnic area at Hemsted Forest, just north of Benenden, with car parking and marked out forest walks as well as the landscaped picnic areas that characterize these Forestry Commission sites, of which Kent has several named or already in use.

Another, nearby, is Bedgebury Forest, the famous and beautiful Bedgebury Pinetum, near Hawkhurst. There, the Commission plans to establish a picnic area on a hill overlooking views right across the Weald. The forest, including the Pinetum, enfolds Bedgebury Park School, established in Bedgebury Manor House which was built in 1688 by Sir James Hayes and paid for with Spanish treasure salvaged from a sunken galleon. Sir James was secretary to Prince Rupert, the Royalist cavalry commander during the Civil War.

The Roman Road linking North Kent at Rochester with the south passed through Iden Green, south of Benenden, and the sandstone stepping stones that marked the ford across the Rother at this point are still to be seen. Another Roman road came westward through Goddards Green, joining the north-south highway in Hemsted Park, and when these roads were excavated comparatively recently, they were found to contain iron slag, spoil from the local foundries that flourished in the Weald even then.

Cranbrook always seems to be a town trying to be a village still—or possibly a village trying to be a town. It did in fact become a market town by royal charter granted by Edward I in 1290 and in the fourteenth century it was one of the first cloth-weaving towns of England, relying on ready supplies of water from springs and streams to power the fulling mills, good timber for the machinery itself, and the fullers' earth that was and still is dug near Maidstone. It is said that the first Queen Elizabeth once walked on a welcoming path of Cranbrook broadcloth a mile long during one of her visits to Kent. But all that was long ago and now you have to detour from the main road (the A229 Maidstone–Hastings road) to visit the village at all. It is completely typically Wealden with its weatherboarded houses and its layout, and it is blessed with a number of those old tongue-in-cheek stories from the past that abound in all the more remote villages everywhere. For instance, it is said that the figure of Father Time on the church clock tower leaves his pedestal at midnight to scythe the grass in the churchyard—a story given no credence at all by those who actually do keep the grass cut. And inside the church is a stone tablet carved with the pedigree of the Roberts of Glassenbury Manor, which is said to have been carved by the wife of the first Duke of St Albans, son of Charles II by Nell Gwynn, to show her husband that her lineage was every bit as good as his.

St Edith's Well, Kemsing

Old houses opposite the church, Chiddingstone

A single oak tree, split in two, forms the entrance to the church of
SS Peter and Paul, Shoreham

One-time home of Anne Boleyn, Hever Castle

Penshurst Place,
family home of the Sidneys.
(*left*) The fountain in the garden.

Cranbrook School, is a public school founded in the sixteenth century and added to (the buildings there today seem to suggest) throughout just about every architectural period ever since, and not always with wholly happy results. Lord Rootes was a pupil at Cranbrook and he has contributed a twentieth-century science block.

A familiar landmark of the village is the smock mill which Henry Dobell built on the hill practically in the centre of the village, and which has been recently restored to working order, although it no longer depends upon wind power. There has been and continues to be a good deal of new building in the Cranbrook vicinity which is, in point of fact, one of the fastest-growing parts of the county.

North from Cranbrook is Sissinghurst, a name that is no older, in its present form, than about 150 years. Before that it was known as Milkhouse Street or Rose Village, because of the number of roses in the cottage gardens there. But Sissinghurst Castle was built during the reign of Henry VIII by Sir John Baker, Speaker of the House of Commons, Attorney-General and Privy Councillor, and it is from the castle that the village has now taken its name. Jeffrey Farnol knew Sissinghurst and wrote the cottages opposite the Bull Inn into his book *Broad Highway*. An even more celebrated visitor to the village was Queen Elizabeth I, who visited the castle in 1573.

During the Seven Years' War, the castle, somewhat decayed by then, was used as a prison for about 3,000 French prisoners of war, and in the nineteenth century it became a poor-house. Then the late the Hon. Sir Harold Nicolson and his late wife, the former Miss Victoria Sackville-West, bought and restored the castle and made its gardens into one of the most delightful attractions of Kent. It is not conspicuously castle-like now, but is instead a very charming residence, with fragments of the Tudor house that survived into the nineteenth century, when it was almost completely demolished. The gardens are open to the public during the summer, and administered by the National Trust.

H

Visitors to the house can climb the spiral stairway in the Elizabethan tower, and look out across what must be one of the most breathtaking views in all England, certainly in the south-east, across the woods and the fields and the hop gardens, all the way over the broad Wealden valley to the North Downs beyond.

But it would be wrong to give the impression that Sissinghurst is nothing but the castle and its gardens; there are shops and the inevitable garages, and the whole village still has a rather neat and tidy appearance as it must have done in the days when it was known by the rather delightful name of Rose Village.

Still further north is the very old little village of Frittenden, first mentioned as Frythingdene and a gift from Kenewulf, King of Mercia. Although a little remote, by-passed at about equal distances by the A262 to the north, the 274 to the east, and the A229 on the west, it is within easy striking distance of the shops and railway stations of Staplehurst and Headcorn, both on the London–Kent coast main railway line. There are a number of well-preserved buildings to attract the eye in and around the village itself.

The first and most obvious one is Frittenden's own church of St Mary, perched on relatively higher ground than the rest of the village, with an unusually slim and elegant spire topping its square tower. There are some very picturesque farmhouses and cottages nearby, too: Lashenden, Ponds and Weaversden, for example, as well as some attractive old oast houses. The old water wheel at Maplehurst Mill no longer turns, but it is still there; whereas nothing but the name, Hammer Stream, remains to recall the days when local industry had need of a water-powered hammer mill as well.

Headcorn is essentially a commuter village on the main London-coast railway line, but its main street, particularly, has kept most of its country village loook, with several prettily half-timbered houses including the unusually tall Shakespeare House. Adjoining the churchyard is the old Cloth Hall, a really fine example of its kind, recalling the village's former importance in the cloth-weaving industry, and behind the church a row of attractive cottages deferentially line the way to Headcorn Manor, built in 1516 for the local parson. Recent growth has treated Headcorn kindly and in fact the village prides itself on the way in which old and new, both residents and their residences, have integrated to retain a harmonious community without the sharp differences so sadly apparent in some much less fortunate commuter villages throughout Kent.

The Danes left very little impression upon Kent. They raided the coast a good deal, occasionally penetrating some miles inland. But they never settled in the county to any great extent and they left few reminders of their having been here. Yet, centuries after the Danes stopped being troublesome, twelfth-century Danish iron-work was used to decorate the very distinctive door of Staplehurst church with iron fishes, snakes and other serpents designed, possibly, to ward off evil spirits. The church register at Staplehurst is, in fact, one of the earliest in the country. Exceptionally, it is written on paper, while most others of this period (mid-sixteenth century) were on parchment. A stone column remembers three Staplehurst martyrs burned at Canterbury and Maidstone in the sixteenth century: Alice Benden, Alice Potkins and Joan Broadbridge.

Staplehurst today is a pleasant village with a number of modern properties vouching for its attractions for newcomers who find its main line station a convenient starting point for the daily commuter-trek to London or the county capital of Maidstone, and a soothing rural retreat to return to afterwards. But there is no denying that the development has not been altogether sympathetic to the old character of the village and, in fact, visually the village is a rather glaring example of what too-rapid, poorly-planned growth can do to an old and well-settled community.

It was the Celts who first began the long civilizing process in Kent. It was they who named the river Beult—it signifies a winding river, which the Beult certainly is—and the river Teise as well

—the stream through the pastures. Both feed into the river Medway at Yalding.

When the Romans came, they camped and perhaps built up a more considerable settlement at Marden, and there was a Roman villa on the northern ridge outside the present village. When the legions went back to Rome, Anglo-Saxon history recorded Marden as Merdenne, which is how it appeared in the Domesday Survey, by which time the village had its own Court House. It still has, although the building is now a shop in what used to be The Green.

Marden enjoyed the distinction of being Crown property longer than any other property in Kent and was, in fact, the main town of the county for many years. It was a Royal Hundred, and therefore exempt from the jurisdiction of the county Sheriff. But in 1607, James I made the village over to Sir Henry Brown, and in 1648 it was bought by the Earl of Pembroke. To this day, though, Marden retains the distinction of having the Archbishop of Canterbury as its Rector.

The church is notable for its rather odd-looking wooden 'snuffer' on the tower, which replaced the original battlements and steeple when the first six bells were hung and the belfrey was weatherboarded. There is a tombstone, half inside and half outside the church, beneath which is buried De Luci, twelfth century Lord Chief Justiciar in the reign of Henry II. The tomb was brought to Marden in the sixteenth century, in secret, after it had been desecrated where it originally was, at Abbey Wood.

It was De Luci, probably the richest man of his day, who drew up the Constitutions of Clarendon in 1164, and brought to a head the two hundred years-old struggle for power between the Church and the state.

It is likely that there was a settlement 400 feet up on the High Weald ridge where Goudhurst now is more than a thousand years ago. But when the Normans began the biggest land-grab England has ever known, they found at Goudhurst just a few wattle and daub huts for the swineherds to whom this was home, and they didn't even bother to jot it down in the records that became the Domesday Book. Within fifty years of the Norman invasion, though, there was a tiny chapel at Goudhurst, from which the present rather lovely church developed.

Goudhurst came into prominence after the fourteenth-century settlement here of Flemish weavers and for the next three hundred years the village prospered from the wool of local sheep. There are still weavers' cottages to be seen there, in Church Road; a row of cottages with undivided attics where the cloth was stretched. In the High Street there are more reminders of this period of prosperity for the village, in the larger houses with loom recesses.

Like many other Wealden villages, Goudhurst divided its industry; by Tudor times the village had joined the Wealden iron smelting centres and the whole countryside around the village is pitted with marl pits from which the ore-bearing stone was quarried. Most of them, today, are disguised as overgrown copses; some are ponds.

Like Hawkhurst to the south, Goudhurst fell into the depression that followed the decline of the weaving and iron-founding industries in the eighteenth century, and fell back upon the increasing importance of the local fruit and hop farming. It was during this period that smuggling flourished throughout the Romney Marsh and the Weald and the real Wild West character of the region flared briefly in Goudhurst in 1747 when the whole area was being terrorized by the notorious gang led by the two Kingsmill brothers, Thomas and George. The reign of terror ended when the Goudhurst villagers formed their own band of vigilantes who shot it out with the gang. In the battle, one of the brothers was killed and the other was hanged a year later. So peace returned to the village where, we can hope that, as in all the best stories of the kind, everyone lived happily ever after!

The next 'invasion' of Goudhurst came in Victorian times, when the village was one of the Wealden centres for the noisy, boisterous and colourful annual hop-picking spree when hundreds of Londoners and their families flocked to the county for the autumnal 'hopping', starting a tradition that lasted until the mid-twentieth century when it was killed off almost abruptly by the hop-picking machines.

Today, Goudhurst is a service centre for a wide surrounding rural area and welcomes to its tea shops and pubs the many visitors who come to see what old Kent looks like. They find, at the top of the High Street, an area that is almost a village square, with a rich variety of building materials and colours and styles, all managing to exist rather cosily side by side. Many of the buildings are listed as of special architectural or historic interest and the church, St Mary's, which is on the highest point but is not particularly prominent because of its squat design, is a Grade A listed church, which makes it really rather special even in the distinguished company of many of its fellows.

Hops could be said to have bought the village of Lamberhurst for Kent. Until the end of the nineteenth century, the village was only partly in Kent. The rest, south of the river Teise, was in Sussex, for the river which flows through the village used to form the county boundary at this point. But when local government boundaries were reorganized in 1894, the village decided it wanted to be wholly Kentish. It is said that the price of hops in Kent was traditionally better than in Sussex and that that was the deciding factor. Well, farming folk have always been a good deal more canny than many townsmen would like to give them credit for, and it would not be very surprising if some such consideration did, in fact, swing the local preference. Whatever the reason, Lamberhurst is now decisively Kentish, and it is now Kent and not Sussex that can claim as its own the iron railings for St Paul's Cathedral which were cast at Lamberhurst. The famous Gloucester Furnace at Lamberhurst, which operated during the seventeenth and eighteenth centuries, was named after Queen Anne's son, the Duke of Gloucester, who visited it with the Queen in 1698.

The road out of Lamberhurst towards Horsmonden passes the thirteenth-century church which has recently been completely renovated, using for the first time in England an Italian reinforcement process for the foundations. The village is an interesting example of how the architecture of different periods can blend together, for the development of Lamberhurst can be traced in the village today from houses dating from the fifteenth century, and featuring typical Wealden styles all the way from half-timbered and weather-boarded houses through tile-hung, brick and stone to today's breeze block and pre-formed concrete.

Nearby Scotney Castle is another of Kent's National Trust properties and definitely a not-to-be-missed delight of south-west Kent. Dating from 1377, there remain some parts of the old castle and there are remains, too, of Tudor and Jacobean buildings. The new house was built to designs of Anthony Salvin in Tudor style, although it was not begun until 1837. Behind the moat, the buildings cluster in picturesque style that never fails to raise a camera lens or two among the many visitors to the house and gardens every summer. For Scotney as it is today we have to thank specially the Hussey family who, for a century and a half have created a living heirloom for the county. The gardens are quite superb in their formal and informal variety, making an almost dreamlike picture of the moated fourteenth-century remains and the adjoining seventeenth-century buildings. The present house overlooks the old one from a vantage point above the gardens and stream.

Of course, quiet serenity is a feature of the Kentish Weald villages; a feature that is being defended vigorously by various organizations and individuals from the assaults of modernity, especially, in many places, modern traffic. But it would be difficult to imagine a more peaceful spot than Horsmonden, between Lamberhurst and Maidstone. Luckily, it stands a very good chance of staying that way, for, like nearby Lamberhurst, it is one of those villages named in the county development plan where new building is very strictly controlled indeed.

Yet, despite the peaceful air of the village, as it clusters round its big old village pub and the tree-girt Heath, Horsmonden once shared in the regional prosperity of the cloth and iron industries and specialized in casting cannon balls for the army. The pub, at least, has not forgotten those days. It is called 'The Gun', and in the adjoining woods there is another reminder of those 'good old days', Furnace Pond.

Nowadays, Horsmonden is almost wholly agriculture-based— hops, fruit, grazing, some cereals—although it has never completely shrugged off its industrial heritage and the long-abandoned skills of the old iron-founders have found fresh expression in their grandchildren who work in the local plastics factory and engineering works.

The village church is another of those that stands some little distance from the village centre. It is an interesting building with a rather handsome Perpendicular tower and a wall tablet commemorating John Read, inventor of the stomach pump.

There is an almost Christmas-card air about Brenchley, even in summer, for fate has decreed that the village shall lie snugly on its steep hillside between Lamberhurst and Paddock Wood, well removed from anything like a traffic-inviting road. It is a well-wooded village; the great Kent topographer, Edward Hasted, thought the number and size of the trees in the neighbourhood made Brenchley a dreary and gloomy place. Perhaps it was in his day. Or perhaps that was just old Edward's personal view getting in the way a bit. Today, at any rate, the trees are a distinct enhancement, helping to mask what would almost certainly otherwise be a rather unfortunate spread of building outward along all the approach roads.

The village green forms the hub of four roads and most of the buildings in this part of the village are listed as of architectural or historic interest, and at least for the present such buildings as the superb Old Palace, the Old Vicarage and the Old Workhouse can brood comparatively peacefully upon four hundred years that have brought very few major changes to the local scene. Outside the village, on a hill, is the site of the former Knowle Castle, marked by what remains of a double ring of defensive earthworks.

About a mile north of the village is the sixteenth-century castellated Moatlands (complete with moat, as you might expect from the name); to the south, Brattles Grange is another six-teenth-century building, this one half-timbered. Just outside the village is a house that may have been the home of the fourteenth-century Kentish rebel, Wat Tyler.

All this part of Kent, of course, is the heartland of the Kentish Weald hop-growing country and the pretty little village of Mat-field is in the midst of the hop gardens, seeming to crowd itself round its village green and its pond as though anxious not to tres-pass on a single precious acre of neighbouring hop-garden or orchard.

The 'big house' at Matfield is Crittenden House, the present owner of which is justly proud of his superb gardens which, each year, he floodlights for visitors who come from far afield to enjoy the spectacle and delight in the quite exceptional beauty of this garden in the Garden of England.

Of course, although almost doggedly rural, the natural attrac-tions of the whole area have inevitably made it a goal for those people who have sought and found here a retreat from which to sally forth to the City and this part of Kent is dotted with blat-antly modern homes, many of them, nevertheless, very beautiful and surely destined to become the picture postcard attractions of centuries to come.

This is certainly true of Pembury, which is not only astride the main A21 London–Hastings road, and about half way between London and the coast besides, but it is also practically on the out-skirts of Tunbridge Wells and within ten or fifteen minutes' drive of the main railway line at Tonbridge.

Even so, the village is certainly not all modern; the eighteenth-century almshouses were built by Charles Amherst to house six old people who were to be nominated by the Marquis Camden, whose family name crops up in the Camden Hotel, which can recall the days when the stage coaches pulled up outside its tile-hung front-age and travellers came through the pillared porches into the warmth and comfort of the bars.

Less old, despite appearances, is the Tudor-style Hawkwell

Place, a nineteenth-century mansion now housing Kent College, a girls' college which moved here from Folkestone in 1939.

The name of Paddock Wood is almost synonymous with Kentish hops. The village is, quite literally, the capital of the hop-growing regions of the county. Yet, until the coming of the railways, Paddock Wood was no more than a hamlet. Today it has, perhaps, already outgrown its entitlement to space in this book. It still is the hop capital of Kent if only because of the Hops Marketing Board store there. But it is much besides that now, with a variety of industries, some, but not all, agriculture based, like the canning factory, for instance. At present, Paddock Wood faces the prospect of booming into an indisputable township of international and especially European renown with the development of the Eurocentre transport depot there. There is little enough of the distant past in and around Paddock Wood that will be harmed by this boom, but there are many conservationists who fear that major growth of Paddock Wood will inevitably lead to a loss of local character beneath the weight of more and more traffic and more and more development. Time will tell.

Five Oak Green, Capel and Tudeley are small villages between Paddock Wood and Tonbridge. Tudeley had a church in Saxon times, although the present one is much later than that, and Capel has a parish church that once belonged to the Knights of St John of Jerusalem, with wall paintings believed to be seven hundred years old.

North of Tonbridge, Hadlow village, although basically very old, is practically all comparatively modern now. As a settlement it dates back to Roman times, and has its place in the Domesday Book (where it is described as Haslow), but it first came to any sort of prominence as a true village after the mid-eighteenth century.

At nearby Golden Green, there is a house, Barnes Place, which traces its origins back to the end of the fourteenth century; and there are some Tudor houses in the village of Hadlow itself, including the King's Head in Church Street, and the Rose and Crown in Ashes Lane. Several of the houses are Elizabethan rebuildings of older homes, and Hadlow Place was rebuilt in 1515.

A prominent landmark from every direction is the tall, slim tower of Hadlow Castle. This 150 foot 'folly' is designed like a telescopic tiered cake, and is almost all that remains of a nine-teenth-century mansion. At one end of the village is Hadlow College, the West Kent agricultural college, and the village is one of several contenders for the title of birthplace of William Caxton, the first English printer.

Deep in the hop-growing country of the Kentish Weald is East Peckham, a quite large village surrounded by several small hamlets and including in the parish the very fine red brick Elizabethan mansion, Roydon Hall, formerly family seat of the Twisdens.

Better-known, although smaller, is Beltring, where the famous Whitbread Hop Farm attracts hundreds of visitors every year to the largest group of oast houses in the county. The oasts are work-ing showpieces and the farm, amid the surrounding hop gardens, is laid out as few farms are, with well-tended grassed areas and a tea-shop and kiosk for postcards and souvenirs.

North of East Peckham, Mid-Kent begins to take over gently from the Weald, and little settlements like Collier Street, Benover, Chainhust and Laddingford could equally be included in either region.

# 6

# *West Kent*

UNTIL the 1965 London government reorganization, there was quite a lot more of West Kent than there is now. The boundary changes that accompanied the creation of the Greater London Council pushed Kent back from such places as Biggin Hill (the famous war-time fighter airfield) Beckenham, Bromley, Orpington and Bexley and, of course, from all the villages that used to lie among them.

For the purposes of this book, it probably matters very little that these villages are no longer in Kent. They are no longer villages in any real meaning of the term. They have been absorbed into the almost uninterrupted townscape that is Greater London. Until that happened, though, this had been London's countryside for centuries. And when London spilled over—as it has been doing steadily, and in spite of the best efforts of sovereigns and Governments, even since the marshes between the City and Westminster were built upon—the countryside continued to be that land which always remained just beyond the new building limits.

More recently, the difference has become firmer, as planning law has defined a Green Belt around the metropolis in which all building is very carefully controlled. Part of that Green Belt includes a very large slice of West Kent. Which is something of a mixed blessing, since it protects what is already there, but only by freezing it into a sort of timeless immobility. And although many conservationists regard that as a sort of ideal to be aimed for in other parts of the county as well, it remains a fact that similar strict controls in the past would have meant that many of those delights we now have in West Kent would have been denied to us. We might wonder if future generations will be quite as grateful to use for preserving the past here in the West Kent green belt, in quite the way we so often expect them to.

However, there is no denying that almost the whole of West Kent is, in the language of planners and estate agents, of very high amenity value, possessed of the two most expensive real estate qualities there are—great visual attractiveness, and complete exclusiveness. Today, some of that exclusiveness and amenity value is surrendered to aircraft noise, which local residents say is a considerable nuisance, and which officialdom tends to shrug off as of very minor consequence. I do not live in West Kent and it may be that my visits have been too brief to force the aircraft noise upon my consciousness. Certainly noise of all kinds is a real and growing intrusion upon the blessed quiet that used to be as natural a feature of rural life as grazing cows and ripening corn. To what extent the noise of aircraft actually does detract from the enjoyment of the rural life perhaps depends very much upon the sensitivities of the local residents.

West Kent, properly, is all that area peopled by the Kentish Men, west of the river Medway. It is considerably less than half the total area of the county and, remembering that, using the river as the dividing line, East Kent includes the giant connurbation of Gillingham and Chatham, as well as the Thanet and Channel ports concentrations and Ashford, West Kent as it now is has fewer people in it, too.

But I do not really think I shall be offending any of the natives, whether the Men of Kent or the Kentish Men, if for present purposes I pull the frontiers of West Kent a few miles west of the river, nearer the A227 from the point where it crosses the A20 at Wrotham Heath, almost due south through Tonbridge and Tunbridge Wells, on its way into Sussex.

The two natural centres of this part of Kent are Sevenoaks and Tunbridge Wells. The northern part of the region is North Downs country, cut by the Darent Valley with its jewel-sharp little panoramas of fields plunging down to the river and, almost immediately, rearing up again to close in the view and limit it to the copses and pastures on the opposite bank.

All the northern part of the Darent Valley, on either side of the A225 south of the M2 is earmarked as a 'playground' area, making use of the old gravel workings that abound, now filled with water, as lakes for fishing, boating and water sports generally. The plan covers an area extending down the valley almost to Sevenoaks itself, and will eventually include nineteen of the lakes, fourteen of which are north of Farningham, in a chain of public leisure parks linked by stretches of protected countryside. The southern end of the region, around Tunbridge Wells, is characteristically Wealden.

It is probably true that there are more really picturesque villages in West Kent than anywhere else in the county—although, of course, every other part of Kent will contest that bitterly! Right on the edge of Sevenoaks, for example, stands the very pretty little village of Seal, on the main A25 road, although the village centre stands some 300 feet up on the greensand ridge that separates the Downs from the Weald and might be miles from a main road for all the impact it has.

Seal looks across the river, a tributary of the Darent, and the railway towards Kemsing, another but larger hillside village that straggles down into the valley towards Kemsing railway station. There are several houses in the village dating from the sixteenth century and the parish church traces its history back to 1115, and probably a couple of hundred years before that.

Even older is St Edith's Well, named after the daughter of King Edgar who was born at Kemsing in 961 and who became Abbess of a convent near the village, where she died in 985. Less than a hundred years ago, the villagers were still drawing all the water they needed from the well, and today it is preserved, by the war memorial, on a grassy green, where it keeps company with a golden-leafed maple tree which was planted to mark the golden jubilee of Kemsing Women's Institute, the oldest in Kent. There was Kemsing Castle at one time, but that has long gone, leaving no trace. Eastwards, right on the A227, is another strong contender for the 'prettiest village in Kent' title. It was, in fact, winner of the West Kent large villages section of the 1973 Kent's Best Kept Village competition. Ightham is certainly one of the oldest of the county's continuously occupied settlements, probably deriving its name from that of the Saxon King of Kent, Ohta, which takes it back to A.D. 645 at least. It has been well protected from sporadic development and few houses have been built since about 1947. Now it looks as though the Metropolitan Green Belt will be extended outwards to scoop Ightham into its protective embrace and make it even more difficult for would-be developers to change the shape of the village.

One of the finest moated houses in all England remains at Ightham Mote. The 'mote' does not refer to the water that surrounds the house, though; it is the handed-down Saxon word for a place of assembly. The house dates from the thirteenth century and is open to the public at specified times.

Much older still are the nearby Oldbury Hill prehistoric earthworks, but they are not as picturesque as the timbered houses in Ightham village—houses like Town House (1480), The George and Dragon (1515), Skinners House (1555) and Old Stones (1560), once the home of Benjamin Harrison the archaeologist.

There used to be an archibshop's palace at Otford, west of Wrotham. The remains are still to be seen there, although parts have been converted into humbler cottages now. The village is graced by a very attractive pond and green where the war memorial stands. The memorial commemorates local dead in the two World Wars, but it might equally serve as a reminder that this was once much disputed territory. The Romans settled here, and there were at least two Saxon battles fought in the neighbourhood.

With a main road and a main railway line running through it, Dunton Green could hardly hope to escape the attentions of the developers and their clients, the commuters. Add its attractive siting on the lower slopes of the Darent valley sides, and less than three miles from Sevenoaks, and you can pretty well judge what to expect of what was once a very small village indeed, but which has now grown considerably.

Riverhead is barely distinguishable from Sevenoaks urban area now. Northwards it reaches out across the river Darent to link up with the extended Dunton Green and Chipstead, and southwards it stretches into the outskirts of Sevenoaks town.

Filling in the triangular space formed by the junction of the A21 with the A25 is Bessels Green, another part of this outer fringe of the Sevenoaks built-up area.

Chevening, though, alongside the very beautiful eight hundred acres of woodland that is Chevening Park, is still small and retains very much the air of knowing its place in the company of The Big House, Chevening Place, seat of the late Earl of Stanhope.

Chevening Place was one of Inigo Jones' early seventeenth-century houses: a red brick building with cream-coloured tiles, to which later wings, including the famous library of more than 13,000 books, have been added subsequently. Charles, third Earl Stanhope, was a disciple of Benjamin Franklin who pioneered the harnessing of electricity. When he died, in 1816, he was buried in Chevening church on Christmas Eve.

Chevening's parish church of St Botolph was built in 1262, and one of its treasures is the rather beautiful and very unusual sculpture by Chantry of a reclining mother suckling her baby.

Just outside the village, immediately south-west of the junction of the A25 with the A21, is the new Dryhill Quarry Kent County Council picnic area, first of several planned by the county council and formed by reclaiming some eighteen acres of old stone quarry. The area was seeded with grasses and wild flowers and before it was officially opened in 1973 it had won a conservation award from the Royal Institution of Chartered Surveyors. It is a

The church and entrance to Hall Place, Leigh

The fifteenth-century Twyford Bridge, Yalding

Birthplace of the English nation, Aylesford

The bridge over the river Medway at East Farleigh

The causeway path in
the stream at Loose

The old English sport of tilting at the quintain is kept alive at Offham

quiet and pleasant place, withdrawn from the main roads; a bit new and raw-looking still, but a good example of what can be done to put wasted land to work for a highly mobile and comparatively leisured public.

In just about a hundred years, Knockholt has emerged from being little more than an inhabited clearing in the remnants of the great south-west Kent forest into its present position as a reasonably large village with many attractive modern homes in and around it.

But there are still plenty of trees in the neighbourhood, including the noted Knockholt Beeches, a clump of old trees which are a well-known local landmark. In the churchyard is one of the oldest yew trees in Kent. It is said to be a century older than the church itself, and that dates from the second half of the thirteenth century.

Knockholt would have been lost to Kent together with other parts of the old Bromley rural district in 1964, but a local petition swayed the bureaucrats, and Knockholt was restored to the county in 1969.

A very pretty little village just south of the A21 road is Halstead. It stands on high ground among woodlands and orchards and a little distance west of the village is Halstead Place School in its beautiful 150-acre park. Sharing the same parish, but a mile from the village, is the Stonehouse Estate, a large modern residential area that is, in a way, the new Halstead.

Easy enough to see why Shoreham is so named, when you know that the word describes a 'steep place'. It is a very old village, straddling the river Darent which is crossed by a bridge in the village centre, and backed by the chalk hills that rear up from the Darent Valley to the east and west. It seems to have succeeded to a remarkable extent in staying aloof, remote almost, from the twentieth-century frenzy, but this is to some extent illusory. So attractive a village has inevitably brought into it a number of 'outsiders' in search of second homes created, often at considerable expense, from converted cottages that might well, in different

I

times, have been lost. These people look upon the village as their adopted home, and exert a great deal of effective pressure to protect it and preserve it as they want it to be.

Shoreham is by no means unique in this, but it is a particularly good example of a feature of country life today which may be viewed with some misgivings. On the other hand, but for the eloquent protectiveness of these non-natives, such villages as Shoreham could hardly hope to escape the not-always-kindly attentions of the developers, so it is a swings and roundabouts situation.

The entrance to the church of SS Peter and Paul at Shoreham is made from the split trunk of a single oak tree, its organ once belonged in Westminster Abbey, and it boasts one of the finest rood screens in England.

Several Kent villages have used neighbouring chalk slopes as natural mounts for turfed crosses cut as memorials to their dead in two world wars; Shoreham is one.

Many famous people have been associated with the village in its long history: Cromwell's General Ireton lived at Sepham Farm; painter Samuel Palmer, poet William Blake, writer and poet Lord Dunsany (who lived at Dunstal Priory); Lord Mildmay of Flete lived in the now demolished Shoreham Place, and local boy Lieutenant Verney Cameron, RN, son of the vicar, led the first European expedition to cross Africa from west to east coasts.

Little Badger's Mount is almost a frontier village now, entrenched behind the woods around Knockholt Station as though defying Orpington to vault the county boundary and bring the practically unbroken north-western sprawl of Greater London homes and industry into Kent at this point. It has not done so yet and, if the Green Belt continues to be safeguarded as it has been—and there is no reason to suppose that it will not, in spite of all the pressures to allow building there—it will not do so.

Immediately south of Swanley, hard against the county boundary which, in fact, has to twitch westward to keeps its hold on the village, is Crockenhill, another of those North Downs excepted villages protected by the Kent Development Plan from all but the most carefully scrutinized building.

There is almost no clear-cut boundary between Farningham and its southern near-neighbour, Eynsford, now. The intervening countryside has become broken with housing. But the village centre at Eynsford is still easily discernable, above the river Darent, which is crossed at this point by a narrow stone bridge and by a ford. The church, with its slender shingled spire, is a natural hub for the nearby timber and brick main street architecture.

Just aloof from the village are the remains of the 30 foot flint walls of the ancient monument of Eynsford Castle whose first owner, William D'Eynsford, quarrelled with Thomas à Becket. When the ill-fated Archbishop was murdered, though, D'Eynsford was so filled with remorse—so the story goes—that he vowed never to live in the castle at Eynsford again.

Further south still, the imposing red-brick building that is Lullingstone Castle stands on the river. Despite the name, it is more house than castle, surrounded by lakes created by the Darent river's water and by sweeping lawns. To one side is the little flint-walled church where generations of owners of the castle have been buried. These included the illustrious John Peche, Sheriff of Kent in 1495, and later, as Sir John, Lord Deputy of Calais; that long-lived courtier Sir Percyvall Hart, and his wife; and Sir William Hart Dyke, friend of Disraeli, who gave the game of tennis the rules he made during his own games on the Lullingstone lawns. The castle achieved a new distinction when Lady Hart Dyke founded a famous silk worm farm there and there are examples of Lullingstone silk products displayed in the house still, although production has for several years been moved to Hertfordshire.

Just above the castle are the excavated remains of Lullingstone Roman Villa, the best of its kind in Kent and one of the best in the country. The site was first occupied in about A.D. 100 and during the next hundred years a house of some importance and magnificence was built here, with tiled steps leading up from the garden, decorated with marble busts (now in the possession of the British Museum).

After the second century, the villa was apparently abandoned until about A.D. 350 and then the beautiful mosaic floor which so delights the many visitors to the villa now was laid.

Lullingstone villa is unique for its Christian chapel which was built in about 380, presumably after the owner at that time was converted. The remains of the villa were first uncovered in the middle of the eighteenth century by workmen digging fence post holes and now, 1600 years after the famous mosaic floor was laid, thousands of visitors come to marvel at it during the summer 'open' season.

Due west of Sevenoaks, Sundridge draws to one side to allow the main A25 to pass through it, over the river Darent and in the shadow of the looming North Downs. This is a Domesday village —it was Sondresse, then—and the manor was granted to the See of Canterbury by Earl Godwin, father of King Harold. Dr Edward Tenison, brother of Lord Tennyson, was rector of Sundridge for many years and the eighteenth-century mansion, Combe Bank, with its distinctive square towers at the corners, now a convent school, was once the property of the Duke of Argyll, who was Baron Sundridge. His son was Lord Ferrers, who earned the dubious distinction of being the last peer of England to be hanged, which he was in 1760, for killing a servant. Before his death at the end of a silken noose, he prophecied that his wife would meet with a terrible end, which she did, burned to death in a tower of their home.

Brasted, which is another village astride the busy A25 Guildford–Maidstone road, has something of the character of a village implanted in parkland. To the north there is the Combe Bank convent school with its surrounding parkland, and on the other side, south of the village, is the Brasted Place Park which almost links up with the fine stretch of countryside that rolls down to Brasted Chart and up to Toy's Hill.

Brasted Place, which is now a church training college, once

housed Napoleon III before he went back to France to become Emperor. Nearby Ide Hill is a renowned beauty spot, much of it owned by the National Trust now, which affords some of the finest views in the county, right across to the South Downs. The height of the village has given to the clock on the village tower the claim to being the highest clock in Kent, which, in turn, gives local wits an excuse to claim that they always have a high time in Ide Hill!

The road that leaves tiny Ide Hill village northwards back towards the A25 passes Emmetts which, together with the sixty acres of farm and woodland and a four-acre shrub garden, are owned by the National Trust, as is also Scords Wood, which curves round the farm to the south.

Is Westerham a village or a town? It ranks as a village in the local authority hierarchy, but with a population of some 4,500 in the whole of the parish to which it gives its name, it is certainly among the most populous of the county's civil parishes, and is on a par with some of its smaller towns. But perhaps more important, it looks like a small town, and it has the general air of being a town, and a very attractive small town, too.

It is a long-established settlement—town or village; the British Museum owns a collection of gold coins found here together with an early Iron age flint money-box—both of which suggest that there was a certain prosperity here even so early in Westerham's history.

At the foot of the hill below Westerham is Quebec House, where James Wolfe, hero of Quebec, was born in 1727. He became part of English military history when he died on the heights above Quebec in Canada at the moment of victory over the French defenders of the city and province. The house, though, stood where it stands today two hundred years before Westerham's most famous son was born in it, although his family made some alterations and more have been made since. But it still contains several relics of the general and the house was bequeathed to the National Trust by a Montreal woman.

Wolfe's statue dominates the little green at the eastern end of the village, standing on its plinth and apparently defying the forces of twentieth-century modernity to come any closer than the busy A25 which already practically laps the bottom of his platform.

Westerham also remembers that it was, too, the birthplace of Dr Benjamin Hoadley, a Bishop of Winchester; home of William Pitt, who lived in Pitt's Cottage now a restaurant; and of another Prime Minister of England, Sir Winston Churchill.

Crockham Hill is another far-famed vantage point—one of several in this part of West Kent—and just outside the village is Chartwell, now owned by the National Trust, but from 1922 until his death in 1964 the home of Sir Winston Churchill. The Victorian country house is a fairly unpretentious building, completely remodelled when the Churchill's took it over in 1922. Today it enshrines much of the character of the great statesman himself: his library, the living-room in which the forcefulness of his powerful personality is stamped as surely as if he were expected back at any moment; the studio where he painted; and the study to which he was in the habit of retiring when great personal decisions had to be made and where he worked at the books that would have earned him literary fame if events had not written him into world history in the way they did. The house and the lovely gardens were bought in 1945 by anonymous friends of Churchill, who presented it to the National Trust.

Nearby Sevenoaks Weald is a pretty village with a pleasant little village green, the whole protected by that exclusive and excluding county development plan designation of an 'excepted village'.

Between Sevenoaks and Tonbridge, but rather nearer Tonbridge, is Hildenborough. The old village centre is still discernible, with its little piece of green and its neat-spired church, but the countryside all around has been fairly well developed with housing estates, and there is no more than a narrow belt of open country now separating the village from the outlying estates of Tonbridge.

Northwards, the village reached out towards the Shipbourne

Forest, one of Kent's largest Forestry Commission tracts, which stretches westward to cross the county boundary into Surrey. Several long-disused hammer ponds remain to remind us that once the Wealden iron industry fuelled its furnaces with the forest trees.

A constant contender for the Best Kept Village title (which it won in 1971) and certainly one of the most attractive villages in Kent is Leigh (pronounced *Lie*). There is a six-acre tree-girt village green, some very attractive old houses, and some much newer but still old-looking houses, and an appealing old church cheek by jowl with the decorative gateway to the two hundred acres of park surrounding Hall Place, the red brick and stone house which is the family seat of Lord Hollenden.

Leigh has escaped any really extensive development, although there has been some new building, inevitably. Mineral springs within the parish are similar to those which made Tunbridge Wells the Regency spa it was in the eighteenth century, but no similar popularity was visited upon little Leigh. However, there were once gunpowder mills in the countryside between the village and Ton-bridge, although these have long since been abandoned.

A typical Wealden village is Chiddingstone, which forms the apex of a triangle of settlements the base of which connects Hever and Penshurst. Chiddingstone may take its name from a huge sandstone mass which stands in the park of Chiddingstone Castle, and which may have been (despite the assurance of good authorities that it was more probably not) the Chiding Stone used in Druidical ceremonies before the Romans arrived. The village has a most attractive main street, with a row of mellow Tudor cottages opposite the church—so attractive, indeed, that the village is entirely National Trust property.

North of Chiddingstone is Bough Beech reservoir, a flooded valley of 280 acres, part of which is a nature reserve. When the decision was taken to create the reservoir, two fine old houses were condemned to death by drowning. In fact, however, they were reprieved, dismantled piecemeal and moved to the Weald and Downland Open Air Museum at Singleton near Chichester in Sussex. There they have been reassembled in their original forms and comprise two of the most important exhibits in this fascinating collection.

Another of those more-than-a-village less-than-a-town communities is Edenbridge, which has been there, some twenty-five miles from London, certainly since the Conquest and most probably since Roman times.

Edenbridge grew up round the crossing of the river Eden, a tributary of the Medway. The tale is told that the stone bridge was built by a Trust set up by two old ladies after they were prevented from crossing the river to go to church because of floods. There has been a succession of bridges since the first, the present one built in 1834, but all have been of stone as required under the terms of the Trust.

Edenbridge parish takes the county out to the Surrey boundary and includes some very lovely old houses, including the old Priest House near the parish church, the Crown Hotel and the Old House at Home Inn.

The tourist in West Kent might almost think there was something not quite fair in the distribution of beautiful villages that has concentrated so many of them in this corner of one county. But, of course, the physical attractiveness of West Kent generally, together with the proximity to London has meant that, for centuries, certain kinds of Londoners have moved out into the Kentish countryside, bringing their wealth with them and with it the creation of the charm and beauty that remains today. It is a continuing process, too, not only for what it brings into the West Kent villages but, equally important, for what it succeeds in keeping out.

Penshurst is not only a very attractive village in itself, set down among pleasant rolling countryside, it is also the historic home of the Sidney family, a family that has played an important role in English history for centuries.

There has been a house of some importance on the site certainly since Domesday (1085), although the first recorded owner was Sir Stephen de Penchester in the late thirteenth century. He was Constable of Dover Castle and Warden of the Cinque Ports. Other owners of what became Penshurst Place have included Sir John de Pulteney, four times Lord Mayor of London in the four-teenth century, and it is his stone house with its magnificent Great Hall that is the south front of today's Penshurst Place.

In the fifteenth century the house belonged to the Duke of Bed-ford and the Duke of Gloucester, brothers of Henry V, and the first Duke of Buckingham's descendants owned it until the third Duke lost his head in 1521 and the King took Penshurst Place for him-self. It was Edward VI who gave it to Sir William Sidney, whose illustrious grandson gave the house its most famous occupant, Sir Philip Sidney, and to whom the present owner, Lord De L'Isle, VC, traces his own descent.

The village of Penshurst probably traces its own descent back to some anonymous Saxons who cleared this particular bit of the Wealden forest where the permanent settlement gradually grew up. It is on the northern edge of the High Weald, overlooking the Medway Valley, where the Medway is joined by its tributary the river Eden. It is a very compact little village: all the old centre which is very picturesque with houses of many styles and periods, lies within 1,000 yards of the church and Penshurst Place, although there has been a good deal of new building outside that grouping. The Castle and the grounds, and the little toy museum there, are all open to the public during the summer months.

Hever's chief claim to fame, too, is its castle. This one-time home of Anne Boleyn was often visited by King Henry VIII before their wedding, but the building itself is interesting, quite apart from such historical associations.

The oldest part of Hever Castle is a fortified and moated farm-house originally built in the thirteenth century. It was two hundred years after that that the Boleyn family built the Tudor house in-side the wall. After the brief flare of notoriety brought by the royal courtship and short-lived elevation of the daughter of the house,

Anne Boleyn, Hever Castle returned to comparative obscurity until 1903 when it was bought by the American-born naturalized Englishman and one-time American Ambassador in Rome, William Waldorf Astor, who was to become 1st Viscount Astor of Hever Castle. He restored the building and enlarged it by building a complete village of Tudor style cottages to provide guest rooms, servants' and other quarters, all connected to each other and to the castle. The grounds were treated to the same elaborate face-lift, with huge quantities of soil and rock moved to create the formal and informal gardens, the maze, and the unusual chessmen clipped from trimmed yew trees. A thirty-five-acre lake took four years to excavate.

In 1963, the village was converted into self-contained flats, but the castle is still the home of the Astor family and achieved a new status as the home of the Lord Lieutenant of Kent when the present Lord Astor succeeded Lord Cornwallis in that office in 1972.

Very much more modest is the little village of Markbeech, almost due south of Hever, and further south still, Cowden reaches out towards the county boundary. In fact, just west of Cowden village, across the line of the old Roman road that now peters out south of Edenbridge, is Basing Farm which enjoys the special distinction of supporting the very spot where the frontiers of Kent, Sussex and Surrey all meet.

Much of Bidborough, at the top of the Medway Valley between Tonbridge and Tunbridge Wells, is new, its residents enjoying one of the finest views of any villagers in Kent, northwards across the wide, deep valley and over the rooftops of Tonbridge to the distant hills on the far side. Bidborough is an old village lingering on beside a Saxon church, but it has to be searched out among all the newer buildings.

From Bidborough, the road into Tunbridge Wells passes through Southborough a small town that overflows southwards into the larger town of Tunbridge Wells itself to form one elongated urban area of residential streets. But just west of the built-up area is

Speldhurst, from which the parish takes its name and in which is included the three small communities of Langton Green, Old Groombridge and Ashurst.

Parts of Langton Green, from Manor Cottage to All Saints Church and the area including The Green and Langton House have been listed as of special architectural and historic interest. The village is on the Tunbridge Wells–East Grinstead road and although there has been a good deal of residential building in the vicinity in recent years, the village still centres on a quite large green surrounded by trees and attractive houses.

Where the countryside around Langton Green merges into neighbouring Sussex are the famous High Rocks, noted beauty spot and popular as a nursery climb for beginners.

Parts of Speldhurst village, too, are listed as of special interest, including St Mary's church, The Cottage and The George and Dragon Inn. Sir John de Fereby, who lived in the village in the thirteenth century, is remembered today in the road known as 'Ferbies'. A relation of William the Conqueror, he pioneered Speldhurst's development by clearing the forest land for farming here.

In the fourteenth century, Sir Thomas Holland, Earl of Kent, farmed the manor, part of which remains today at Hollonds Farm, near Langton Green. Much of the rest has been swallowed up in the neighbouring Royal Borough of Tunbridge Wells.

It is said that another Speldhurst resident, Sir Richard Waller, Sheriff of Kent in the reign of Henry VI, captured the brother of the Duke of Orleans at Agincourt and held him prisoner in near-by Groombridge for twenty-five years. When the prisoner was finally ransomed, the money went towards rebuilding Speldhurst church, which still has the Arms of Orleans incorporated in the 'Orleans Stone' over the church porch.

Groombridge is rendered schizophrenic by the county boundary. The Kent part of the village is the older part, with a small triangular green overlooked by a picturesque group of tile-hung cottages and a small seventeenth-century brick church. Groombridge Place is a very elegant seventeenth-century moated manor house said by some to have been designed by Wren, although the claim is open to considerable doubt. It has a very charming terraced garden, which is not, however, open to the public.

On the Sussex border, Ashurst is a river Medway village—a very different river, though, from that below Maidstone, with low, wooded banks on either side of a small, pretty waterway. The village's fourteenth-century church has a timbered tower and, in the churchyard, there is an early seventeenth-century sundial which has been mounted on the shaft of an earlier cross.

## 7

# *Mid-Kent*

J U S T as East Kent wheels out from Ashford, so Mid-Kent centres upon Maidstone, the capital town and administrative centre of the whole county. The offices of Kent County Council are in Maidstone. So are the head offices of most of the county organizations and many county, regional and national concerns have their local or branch offices in Maidstone. Not surprisingly, therefore, although the town has a reasonable amount of industry, too, by far the greatest number of the people who live and work in the town and its immediate surrounds spend their days in offices of one sort or another.

Maidstone itself continues to ripple its way out into the rural areas and it is likely to go on doing so for some time to come yet, since regional planning policy provides for the town to accommodate a large part of the expected growth of the county population in the next twenty years or so. There is a weekly market every Tuesday, good shops, two railway stations linking the town with London and the North and South Kent coasts, and generally Maidstone makes a natural nucleus for the villages around, both for shopping and entertainment, as well as for employment.

But by no means all the villagers look to Maidstone for work. More and more of them, since the war, have joined the tide of commuters travelling into London every day and out again to their country homes in the evening to restore themselves ready for the same trek next morning. Others find their daily work in the North Kent industrial areas of Thames-side and the Medway Towns.

Mid-Kent generally is a very attractive part of Kent; many of the villages enjoy truly spectacular views of the North Downs or the Weald—some even enjoy both at once. There are hops and orchards and woodlands and general farmland, and more rivers than anywhere else in Kent, with the Bourne, the Tiese, the Beult and the Len all flowing into the Medway south of Maidstone.

It is because it is so attractive in so many ways, of course, that the area generally has attracted such a large number of 'strangers' to the villages, most of which have long ago lost the very close, almost exclusive, links with local farming that once characterized them.

Very strict planning policies have been applied to some of the villages, virtually embalming them within planning regulations, but others have been allowed to grow until some of them present the appearance of housing estates among which the original village centres are almost completely lost to everyday view.

It is difficult not to feel a little sad when this happens, although it is easy, too, to overlook the fact that what has been lost was not always of such great beauty or value as memory or imagination suggests. Nor is it necessarily to be deplored that what was a small village offering very little in the way of modern amenities to a dwindling number of residents has become a lively socially aware community.

Often, the new building harmonizes reasonably well and the 'newcomers' (who may be second or even third generation villagers now!) are as zealous to protect their environment, and in many cases far better equipped to do so, both financially and influentially, than the older 'locals' might ever have hoped to be.

What is much more important than preserving the past is protecting the future by ensuring that the villages we leave to the twenty-first century are as interesting and as attractive and as functional as those that the seventeenth, eighteenth and nineteenth centuries left for us. Part of that interest and attractiveness is achieved by the variety of period styles that have grown old, side by side, and it may be that future generations will thank us more for conscientiously enlarged villages than for a large number of time-moated anachronisms more suited to museums than to the needs of everyday life.

Throughout Mid-Kent, more than in East or West Kent and much more than in the Weald, the villages have a functional look that owes a great deal to the process of development that has gone on steadily over the years. It may be that developments in East Kent during the next few years will rob that statement of some of its truth, but Mid-Kent is surely destined to reflect the changing face of the county as a whole with the same accuracy that it always has, simply because of its geographical situation.

Like any other region, Mid-Kent is ill-defined and wherever I draw the boundaries for my present purpose I shall be criticized. Local government reorganization might have been said to have solved the problem to some extent by joining the old Hollingbourne and Maidstone rural districts with Maidstone borough into the new Maidstone district, except that this alliance coldshouldered the old Malling rural district on the west and left Maidstone not really a centre of the new district, but rather a western outpost.

No doubt, the North Downs escarpment to the north fairly clearly defines that limit of Mid-Kent, but the other edges blur into East Kent, West Kent and the Weald, with no wholly satisfactory natural breaks to separate them. Certainly, Mid-Kent includes part of the Vale of Holmesdale which follows along the foot of the North Downs escarpment from west to east of the whole county, just as surely as it overlaps the Hythe beds greensands that are responsible for the richness of the Mid-Kent fruitgrowing areas; just as surely as some parts of Mid-Kent are physically in the Low Weald.

The spheres of influence of Maidstone and Ashford overlap

on a line between Charing and Biddenden; east of the line the villagers tend to look towards Ashford, while to the west, Maidstone's magnetism tends to be the stronger. To the south, Maidstone surrenders its influence over the villages to Tonbridge and Tunbridge Wells and to the west, Sevenoaks and London itself reach out more and more strongly.

Like most towns today, Maidstone has reached and physically enclosed several of its closest neighbouring villages. Tovil, for instance, is now wholly within the town's boundaries. It never was a large village, but there is a pleasant little church and a few attractive middle-aged houses among the industry that has settled there. Tovil 'treacle mines' are a well-worn local joke that have been developed over the years into a quite elaborate fable, abetted by newspaper articles and letters to the Press on printed 'Tovil Treacle Mines' headed notepaper.

The approach to Maidstone from the north brings motorists along the A249 Sittingbourne–Maidstone dual-carriageway road that links the town with the M2 motorway.

It is necessary to divert into Stockbury, a tiny, high village that is a memorial to a Kentish saint. St Simon Stock, a twelfth-century hermit who is said to have lived in a hollow tree stump for twenty years. He became head of the Carmelite Order in Europe and lived for one hundred years. Today, the tower of the village church is clearly visible from the Stockbury viaduct that carries the M2 over the Stockbury valley, but as you drop down on to the dual carriageway A249 for the drive into Maidstone, the church drops like a setting sun behind an apple orchard.

The church is about half a mile outside the village centre, around the small triangular village green that is overlooked by the pub, and always seems to greet visitors with that air of hurt surprise that is sometimes seen on the faces of children who are found during a game of hide and seek.

From Stockbury, a road meanders westwards through Yelsted on its way to Bredhurst, hemmed in by two bridges over the M2

'Mighty Mynn' immortalized in the village sign, Bearsted Green

A picturesque corner of Lenham village

St Clement's Church, Old Romney

Newchurch is a typical Romney Marsh village

The steeple of Brookland's Church is in the churchyard

Appledore's village blacksmith stil[l] finds customers for his craftsmans[hip]

'The Woolpack', Warehorn, recalls the great days of the Romney Mar[sh] wool smugglers

almost beside the box junction that links the motorway with the main A2 link at Gillingham.

On the other (eastern) side of the A249 lie Hucking and Bicknor. The first is little more than a hamlet, very closely tied to its agricultural setting, and the second, although larger, is also very strongly agricultural in character. The church of St James, Bicknor, among the orchards outside the village, is very small with a squat tower and a low, slated spire. A close neighbour of the fifteenth-century Bicknor House is what must surely rank as the ugliest oast in all Kent: a cowering building with two flint kilns and red corrugated iron roofs.

Overlooking the Pilgrims' Way, Thurnham has frankly very little to offer visitors, except a really superb view across the Medway valley, and the grave of the famous Alfred Mynn (Mighty Mynn), the Kent cricketer who died in 1861 and whose better-known memorial is in the adjoining parish of Bearsted where the sign on the village green depicts the top-hatted batsman defending his wicket against all-comers.

Thurnham castle, built during the first flush of Norman castle building in England, exhibits a few remains for the determined discoverer—enough, though barely, to justify Thurnham's inclusion in books of reference to English castles.

The A249 road flanks the old Battle of Britain Detling airfield, and the present Kent County Showground before it drops down Detling hill, by-passing Detling village. The bus still diverts into the village, though: a two-part village with attractive old timbered houses around the pub, the Cock Horse (a reminder of days when horse-drawn traffic needed an extra horse—the 'cock' horse—for the climb up the steep hill), and a neat-looking little church that has its churchyard split into two parts on either side of the bus route; and a residential extension of twentieth-century homes pushing out into the fields between the village and Maidstone.

Bearsted, too, comes close to meeting the outskirts of the county town and in doing so, it has stretched itself outwards from the old centre round the large village green which is overlooked

K

by the white cowls of an attractive group of oast kilns. This was where that Mighty Mynn, The Lion of Kent, set up a record which I believe remains unequalled today when he hit a ball from the centre of the green over the neighbouring brewery, across some gardens and into a field beyond. If anyone did equal that feat today, the chances are the ball would drop through a roof that was not there when Mynn toook the field.

But Bearsted no longer clusters round the green alone; it has broken out in estate-type housing in all directions and along the Ashford Road out of Maidstone a linked yet distinct part of the village has grown up, with its own parade of shops, in the vicinity of 'The Yeoman' public house.

Northwards from the A20, a local road winds into Holling-bourne, a very long strung-out village with two distinct groupings of population which, here too, distinguish the original old village from the newer estate-type developments at the northern end. The two halves are separated by the railway, which crosses over the road by a bridge. The northern end of the village ends almost abruptly at the foot of the Downs, just below where the old Pilgrims' Way wends towards Canterbury.

The opposite side of the A20 falls away into Leeds, a very old village where the site of the former Priory can still be seen. The principal architectural interest of Leeds, though, is the castle, with its moat formed from a lagoon fed by the river Len. The castle was built originally by the Saxons, but when the Normans came they enlarged it and from that time on Leeds Castle contributed its periodic paragraphs to the county—and, indeed, the national— history.

It has housed royalty, however reluctantly—Richard II was once imprisoned in Leeds Castle, and so was Henry IV's wife. Later, Eleanor of Gloucester, aunt of Henry VI, was sentenced to life imprisonment in Leeds Castle for witchcraft and treason. French and Dutch prisoners of war have also been lodged at Leeds, and one of the castle's many distinguished owners was that member of the Culpeper family who was Governor of Virginia in 1680.

Westward, the road roller-coasters through woods and farm-lands to by-pass Harrtisham, one of those villages that present one face to the hurrying main-roaders and a very different one to the traveller who will take time to deviate just a little. The A20 road passes through a Harrietsham that is busy and untidy-looking with garages and shops and an old brick-built primary school. But just behind the road, the real village dozes peacefully enough on its changing levels, terraced into the rising Downs and backed by such coy attractions as Coles Dane and Stede Hill (formerly Harrietsham Place) alongside the Pilgrims' Way which invites walkers to see the wide sweep of the Len and Medway valleys from those same vantage points that men have known for thousands of years.

The nearest neighbour of Leeds Castle is not, in fact, Leeds village, but the little hamlet of Broomfield, just to the south. Not a specially distinguished little community, you might suppose, passing through it; but in fact it is the burial place of General Lord Fairfax, one of Cromwell's most prominent generals, who lived at Leeds Castle. After he lost his considerable wealth and high position in the Commonwealth, Lord Fairfax expressed a wish to be buried in a pauper's grave at Broomfield—and so he was.

South again, Kingswood sits back from a country lane forming a cross of estate houses among the surrounding woodlands. Twelve years ago, Kingswood was a hamlet of about forty people. Now a new estate of some 150 homes has created a true village-size settlement of about four hundred people. The village pub has an unusual name, 'The Battle of Britain', a fitting reminder of the battle that was fought in 1940 over all this part of Kent.

Lenham is about as near as we can get these days to turning aside out of the twentieth century and slipping back three, four or five hundred years. It is a typically medieval village, built round a square, the sides of which are closed by old, timbered buildings, and by a church that really looks as though it couldn't be anywhere else. No wonder Lenham holds a 'medieval fair' every year.

At one corner of Lenham Square is the Saxon Pharmacy, named

after a Saxon grave discovered during restoration of the old building, a fine old timber-framed Wealden house with a kingpost
roof. The most distinctive of the square's buildings is the Dog and
Bear Inn, with the royal arms over the door commemorating
Queen Anne's stay there. The church has a number of interesting
features, not least the tombstone of Mary Honeywood, who died,
aged 92, in 1620 leaving no fewer than 367 descendants.

The village has not, naturally enough, considering its siting,
avoided modernization, and there are several estates of modern
houses. The village has also lent its name to the new Freightflow
depot for the trans-Continental T.I.R. lorries. Lenham, incidentally, is one of several Kent villages with a war memorial cross
turfed out of the chalk slopes of neighbouring fields. The cross is
tended by the people of the village and forms a very prominent
landmark, visible from afar.

South of Lenham, the little village of Sandway forms a boundary marker for the Mid-Kent I have chosen, from where to turn
westwards again to seek out Boughton Malherbe, one of four
different Boughtons in Kent and probably named after a Norman
owner of the manor. There is no village, as such, although there is
a church to supplement the few farm buildings that remind us
that here was once the Elizabethan mansion of the Wotton family,
birthplace of Sir Henry Wotton, the sixteenth-century diplomat.

Although firmly within the Mid-Kent region, Ulcombe is un-
arguably Wealden in character, and on the line of what may once
have been a road to Canterbury, although there is very little evidence of the road today. The village makes its voice heard in many
parts of Kent, for it was just outside Ulcombe that the master
bell-founder Joseph Hatch lived. He cast a great many of the bells
that still hang in steeples all over southern England.

East Sutton is almost wholly East Sutton Park and the H.M.
Borstal Institution in it. The park was once a Royalist stronghold
owned by the Filmer family, who were besieged in the house by
General Fairfax during the Civil War. The house fell to the in-
vesters and Sir Robert Filmer was imprisoned in nearby Leeds

Castle. The church at East Sutton contains several Filmer family memorials, including a stained-glass portrait of the last baronet, Sir Robert Filmer, full length and in full-dress uniform. The family died out when he was killed during the First World War.

The A274 which links Maidstone with Headcorn and Biddenden goes through Sutton Valence, which is poised on an almost precipitous slope above the Beult valley and is, in fact, built in terraces down the side of the hill. The most important public building is the public school that takes its name from the village. Sutton Valence School was founded by local clothmaker William Lambe in 1576. It was the same William Lambe that gave his name to London's Lamb's Conduit Street, a reminder of when this benefactor brought fresh water to Holborn in 1577.

Through Chart Sutton and Langley, the road arrives at Otham, an attractive village with a number of half-timbered houses and a particularly fine fifteenth-century house, Stoneacre, which is owned by the National Trust and opened to the public once a week. It was restored in the 1920s. The village is noted as the burial place of William Stevens, founder of the Society of Nobody's Friends in 1800. Stevens was a philanthropist and writer, and the Society still exists today.

The road out of Maidstone to the south forks before it leaves the town behind, into the A274 Sutton Road, which is the one we have just travelled from south to north, and the A229 Loose Road, which carves through the very beautiful Loose Valley towards Staplehurst and Cranbrook in the Weald.

The Loose Valley is one of those parts of the Mid-Kent countryside the region most often and with best reason boasts about. It has been designated an area of outstanding natural beauty; its sides are clothed in woodlands and little, tucked-away fields that all seem to slope eagerly down towards the twin streams that flow along on either side of the built-up pathway through Loose village.

It is a quiet and comparatively little-used area, creating an L-shaped landscape feature of particular local character; a natural corridor running east-west between Boughton quarries and Loose village, and south-north between Loose village and the river Medway at Tovil and Maidstone town.

The valley is up to half a mile wide and the stream widens in places to form small ponds. Once it provided power for old industrial mills, but now there is only one remaining alongside Hayle Mill Road and still in production. Others have been converted into homes, a popular and kindly fate for many one-time industrial buildings in the countryside. As well as the mill, there is a canning business in the valley and several small industries of various kinds all providing the area with a degree of self-sufficiency.

The National Trust now owns the Old Wool House in Well Street at Loose, a reminder that the village once shared the prosperity of the Wealden wool industry. Besides, several groups of buildings in the village have been brought under the protection of designation as areas of special architectural or historic interest, including the old village centre round the green and the stream and the built-up area west of Bottlescrew Hill.

West of Loose is Boughton Monchelsea, still in the Loose Valley and a very scattered community that could claim any one of three or four points as its centre. The Roman habit of leaving evidence of their stay in the vicinity applied here and the south-east corner of the parish is crossed by a Roman road from Rabbits Cross to just past the Chart Sutton road junction.

It was from the Boughton Monchelsea quarries that the ragstone was taken for Westminster Abbey, and just to make sure the supply did not run out during the contract, it was forbidden to take any stone from the quarries for any other purpose until the Abbey had been completed. Much earlier, a Roman temple where St Paul's Cathedral now stands was built of Boughton Monchelsea stone, and other historic uses to which ragstone from these quarries have been put included 7,000 stone cannon balls for Henry V, and repairs to the Houses of Parliament after the 1940 'blitz'. A curious little sidelight on the village is provided by the story that the first known book of French grammar was written for Lady Dionysia de Monchelsea, a member of the family that gave its name to the village.

Continuing south, Linton is another picturesque old village with some nicely grouped medieval buildings that include the 'Bull Inn'. Linton Park, formerly Linton Place and before that Capell Court, was occupied by the Capell family during the reign of Henry VI. The house fell to the Cromwellians during the Civil War and was later demolished to clear a place for the building of the present house in about 1750. The house and park is now owned by the Cornwallis family.

The main road through the village divides the two parts of Linton Hospital and just outside the village is Goosewell, a corruption of Holy Ghost Well, which until 1920 was one of the main sources of the villagers' water supply, and a reputed cure for all sorts of sicknesses.

Once out of Linton, the road plunges into the north Weald where the largest groups of buildings are no more than small hamlets that give the impression of having been yielded, grudgingly enough, by the otherwise unrelieved agricultural land that stretches in every direction, all the way down to Staplehurst or Marden.

North-west of those two major villages, are several small villages, including Collier Street, Benover, Chainhurst, Laddingford and Hunton. Hunton was originally called Huntingston—hunters' town—and the parish includes a fine old Tudor house, Stonewell Farm, notable for having one of the largest fireplaces in Kent, more than 18 feet wide.

Its reputation as a haunt of footpads and smugglers well behind it now, Coxheath is doing its best to outgrow village status and become a small country town. The old village centre has long since been swamped completely by modernity, brought by the large number of estate developments all around it, which in turn has brought upon the village the distinction of having one of the largest and most modern primary schools in Kent. Although most of the new residents commute to Maidstone, the Medway Towns or

London, Coxheath is still a very rural-based community, and quite a lot of the people who live there follow the village tradition and work on neighbouring farms.

Where the Teise and the Beult run into the Medway, south-west of Maidstone, is Yalding, a two-part village held into a single unit by its High Street.

Yalding is dominated by the river. In the summer, the whole area around the lock teems with people messing about in boats or watching other people messing about in boats. It is a starting point for many a river Medway holiday cruise and there is some boat-building there, too. Plans exist for the development of the whole riverside area at Yalding to become Kent's leading water leisure centre.

The river Beult actually divides the village into its two parts, and a fifteenth-century stone bridge joins the two parts together again. The bridge is the longest of its kind in Kent, with a shop and a house in the middle. It is something of a tourist attraction itself, although less than ideal for modern traffic.

The main part of the village lies on higher ground, north of the river. This is where the church is; so is Court Lodge and Cleaves House which was originally a seventeenth-century grammar school founded by a London haberdasher, William Cleaves, in 1663. At the turn of the century, there was an outbreak of new building south of Vicarage Lane which brought the present school to the village, and the Baptist church. There has been some estate-style building since then, too.

Downstream, at East Farleigh, is another magnificent five-arch medieval bridge, one of the best in southern England, marking the spot where Cromwell's General Fairfax crossed the river before the Battle of Maidstone in 1648, when the Royalist town fell to the Parliamentarians after a short, sharp fight that remains one of the highlights of local history.

Queen Elizabeth gave to the townsmen of Maidstone the liberties of the Medway water from East Farleigh Bridge downstream to Hawkewood, and one of the 'liberties' enabled the Corporation to keep swans on this stretch of the water and to use their own mark to identify their swans.

Neighbouring West Farleigh is much less a village, although there is a village green and a public house at each end of the road. The people that make the straggle of habitation a village community are spread through the surrounding farmlands in small groups of cottages, creating a very sweeping, uncluttered countryside unusual this far west. Locals say the village cricket ground is the most beautifully situated in Kent and, despite similar claims by other villages, they might be right at that.

Like a last outpost of Maidstone, Barming clings to the western rim of the town's built-up area and in spite of the very considerable number of new homes in and around the old village area, Barming retains many of the features of a true village. The church boasts some superbly carved, six hundred-years-old Flanders bench ends in the choir stalls and its village inn, 'The Bull', still manages to look as though it were the centre of village life. The old Barming bridge over the river Medway collapsed under the weight of a traction engine in 1914, and now St Helen's Bridge has the distinction of being the only wooden bridge over the navigable length of the river.

The Tonbridge Road goes through Teston (pronounced *Teeson*, please!) half-way up the steep slope of the southern side of the Medway valley, and overlooks another of those fine medieval stone bridges that bejewel the thread of the river between East Farleigh and Yalding. Teston has its own local industries, including the making of cricket balls, one of very few places in the country where the craft lives on. What would happen to the English national game if the skills of cricket ball manufacture should be lost does not bear thinking about for so far no-one has been able to make machinery that will do the job as well as the craftsmen do it by hand.

A former Lord Mayor of London once lived at Wateringbury and he was responsible for having some of the old stonework of Old London Bridge brought from London by barge to the village where it can be seen today in Pelicans, the oldest building in the parish. Wateringbury has another distinguishing possession: a Dumb Borsholder, a unique relic of the symbol of authority of the Hundred Courts. It is an oak staff, with an iron point at one end and a ring at the other.

South of Wateringbury is Nettlestead, the only village in the old Maidstone rural district to be included among the Kent Development Plan designated 'excepted villages' in which all development was to be most carefully controlled. Nettlestead was once the home of the Sir Thomas Scott who led the 4,000 Men of Kent contingent that helped to defeat the Spanish Armada. More recently, the village has invested in future fame by becoming the first of several twentieth-century revivals of the ancient vineyards of southern England to operate commercially. Now the vines at Cherry Hill produce a very distinctive and authentic Kentish wine.

Just north of the point where the A26 fishtails, one branch continuing eastwards back into Maidstone and the other striking north to West Malling, is the little village of Mereworth which although very prettily situated is not specially distinguished. However, it does borrow reflected glory from nearby Mereworth Castle, a private house recognized as probably the most perfect example of English building in the eighteenth-century Palladian style. It was built for the Earl of Westmorland and accounts for the lack of very old buildings in Mereworth village. The original village, including the church, was demolished to make room for the mansion. The new church, with its ornate steeple rising above the trees, looks completely out of place in its rural setting.

North-west of the village, Mereworth woods spread over the countryside in a reminder of the great forests that once covered all south-east England.

West Peckham has nothing in common apart from the name with East Peckham. The two are several miles apart and the former is much smaller than its eastern counterpart. Set aloof from the main roads, West Peckham rests in peace among its farmlands, a pleasant little backwater of a village.

But not far from the village centre is Dukes Place, once a property of the Knights Hospitallers and prominent vantage points from which to enjoy views over the surrounding countryside include Gover Hill, an area of National Trust woodland, and The Hurst.

On the A227 northwards out of Tonbridge, Shipbourne has given its name to one of Kent's three Forestry Commission forests, which stretches away westward, bitten into by the Sevenoaks urban area, but continuing past Westerham and across the county boundary into Surrey. Shipbourne village is still predominantly agricultural in character, as it was in the eighteenth century when the poet Christopher Smart, who was born here, wrote his long definitive blank verse treatise on hop growing, which he called quite simply "The Hop Garden".

There is a large common and part of the Fairlawne estate lies within the parish of Shipbourne. The estate was formerly the seat of the Vane family, one of whose members, Sir Henry Vane, was executed on Tower Hill in June 1662, and whose headless body was interred in the church crypt.

Fairlawne House, former home of that Sir Harry Vane who was Governor of Massachusetts, is north of Shipbourne village in the neighbouring parish of Plaxtol, which also includes a famous eighteenth -century farmhouse, Old Soar Manor, with the preserved original solar building of a thirteenth-century fortified house, now belonging to the National Trust.

There are several fine old buildings in the Plaxtol neighbourhood: Old Basted and Little Damas are both half-timbered Elizabethan houses; Spout House was built before that, in the fourteenth century; and the old forge, now a restaurant, is fifteenth century.

Fairlawne is a well-known racing stable, where horses owned by many famous people, including members of the Royal Family, have been trained.

There is very little about Borough Green that marks it out as a village at all. It does not look like a village, but it is; a small but busy village at the junction of the important A25 Maidstone–Reigate road and the spur road to the A20 London–Folkestone road. There is, in fact, no green at Borough Green. The village sits on a hump of ground, full of activity and small industry that includes brick works, sand excavation, stone quarries, light engineering and distribution centres. There is a large bus station, and a railway station that has encouraged commuter-building which has added to the general air of purpose that Borough Green seems to have.

Much more village-like though, is the very old settlement of Wrotham (pronounced *Rootham*) where the remains of the former Archbishop's palace can still be seen just east of the present church. The village was given to the monks of Christ Church, Canterbury, in 964 by Ethelstan, King of Kent. Most of the palace was pulled down during the reign of Edward III and the materials taken to Maidstone where the new palace was built beside the river. It still stands today. Henry VIII spent a night at the manor house of Wrotham Place, while he was waiting for news that Anne Boleyn had been executed. Wrotham church is distinguished by having in its tower a clock that is at least 350 years old, and one of the oldest in the country. But the district is no longer noted as it once was for Wrotham slipware, which was made of local red clay decorated with white pipe clay.

Once part of Wrotham parish, Platt broke away and became an independent parish, including Crouch, Wrotham Heath and Great Comp among its hamlet population. Platt village once shared in the Wrotham potteries industry. Great Comp is a fine old house with a garden which is open at certain times during the year.

Climbing out of Wrotham, northwards, the traveller comes to Stansted, which reaches thickly wooded heights of up to 700 feet. Today's village retains little enough to remind visitors or residents either that it was a borough and a place of some importance as long ago as the fourteenth century, when the residents had the right to hold a three-day fair there. There is a yew tree in the churchyard which is said to be more than 1,000 years old and Soranks Manor at nearby Fairseat was built on the foundations of an old medieval manor house.

Offham is a village that always looks as though it never set out to be anything but a guide book cover. It has had plenty of time to make up its mind about that, too, because the village history began with the date A.D. 832 when Kent's King Ethelwulf gave it to the church at Canterbury. At that time it was called Ofnehamne.

Today, it is a picturesque village in that part of Kent into which it is proposed to extend the Metropolitan Green Belt, and county planning policy includes Offham among those villages where the present shape and size will be preserved by confining all new building to inside the present village area.

There is a fine group of half-timbered cottages round the village green, where stands England's last remaining quintain, a sort of weathervane with a small weight hanging from one end of the vane. This piece of medieval apparatus was once used for the ancient sport of tilting at the quintain, in which horsemen charged the flat, unweighted end of the vane with a tilting lance, the object being to gallop past faster than the vane could swing round and cuff the rider with the weight on the other end. The sport is still practised—in less robust fashion—as part of the annual jollifications in the village. Today though, cricket has taken over as the major local sport and Offham is another of those several Kent villages claiming to have the most picturesque cricket ground in the county.

Between the A25 and the M20 lies Addington, another Domesday survivor, only then it was known as Eddingtune. The fourteenth-century inn, 'The Angel', is one of the attractions of the village, and there are other fine old buildings round the village green.

Another of those villages where new development is being very strictly controlled, Addington was, in 1972, winner of the West Kent small villages section of the county's Best Kept Villages competition, the prize for which was a wooden seat that now commemorates the victory on East Street Green. Addington is on the site of a prehistoric settlement, and a megalithic long barrow and pre-historic burial chamber are among the local sights.

West Malling really is no longer a village, since the extensive new estate development arrived in the immediate vicinity. Its original centre, in any case, charming though it still is, lacks the cosy intimacy of smaller villages; the main street is exceptionally wide, and flanked with solid-looking frontages that would not be out of place in a prosperous town. However, it is still, technically, a village, with a long and close involvement with the area. Nearby Banky Meadows are said to be where the very many residents who died during the fourteenth century Black Death visitation were buried, and the old village was destroyed, together with West Malling Abbey, in 1190. The Abbey was rebuilt as one of England's first Norman nunneries and had a chequered career, largely subject to the politics of successive owners. Today, the Abbey is in two parts; one is occupied by Anglican Benedictine nuns and the other by Anglican Cistercians.

Just south of the village the neighbouring hamlet of St Leonards includes St Leonard's Tower, one of the finest and perhaps the first of the Norman keeps (dating from about 1080) remaining in England. It was once part of the manor house of Bishop Gun-dulph of Rochester. More recently, it was used as a prison and then a hop store. Now it is fully retired and open to the public, free, at all times.

The age of this part of the county as a human settlement is evidenced everywhere. In the village main street the Bear Hotel is part Tudor, part Georgian; 'The Swan' is eighteenth century; Malling Place is Elizabethan and The Manor House is Georgian, like Malling House, Brooke House and New Barns. There is Nor-man stonework in the kitchen behind one High Street shop and Market Cross Cottage has a medieval upper part. Ford House has a six hundred-year-old wattle and daub wall inside it, and Yew Tree Cottage at St Leonards dates from the fourteenth century.

During a long history, West Malling has been known for a number of industries, including tanning, brewing, quarrying, glass-blowing, clock-making and even straw hat making. Today it is a mainly agriculture-based village, although most of its residents travel to work either in London or Maidstone or the Medway Towns.

In the Second World War, West Malling aerodrome was a famous Battle of Britain airfield, and there is still an RAF station there today. The field has recently been bought by the Kent County Council, although its future is not yet certain. During the Ugandan-Asians' expulsion in 1972, large numbers of the new arrivals to England were temporarily housed in disused married quarters on the airfield, which was one of the last of the Ugandan Asian camps all over the country to disperse its refugees. A short distance from the village, too, is the King Hill Kent County Council hostel for homeless families.

Moving in towards Maidstone along the A20, Leybourne stands demurely aside on the left, a mere shadow of its former self when it was a place of some importance as the home of the de Leybourne family, who had a Norman castle there. Sir William de Leybourne was the first English admiral, and his grand-daughter, Juliana, became known as the Infanta of Kent because of her great wealth. Only fragments of the old castle stonework remain in the village today, built into a modern house, one-time home of Sir Joseph Hawley who distinguished himself by owning no fewer than four Derby winners.

Leybourne church is a pleasant but undistinguished building from the outside, with a square tower capped with a pyramidical roof. Inside, though, is a unique (to this country) double-heart shrine. One of the twin shrines has never been used, but the other is said to contain the heart of Roger de Leybourne, a Crusader who died in Palestine in about 1271.

Closer in towards Maidstone, Larkfield is basically an old village which has put on a lot of weight in recent times. Alongside the A20 itself, the village is characterized by shops and filling stations, but just north of the road there is a quite large development of estate homes and council houses, with their own schools, fire station and shopping centre, so that it is virtually a new and complete village. The growth of Larkfield is partly the result of its convenient siting as a commuter village, but much more the result of the growth of local industries.

Just to the north, at New Hythe, is the Reed Paper Mill, the largest in Europe and almost a village in itself, lacking only its own on-site workers' homes.

Between Larkfield and New Hythe is another very new industrial development in a former sandpit, where the industrial estate that is growing up includes the printing works and head offices of Kent's largest newspaper group, the Kent Messenger Group.

Almost directly opposite Larkfield on the other side of the A20 is East Malling. The two villages are, in fact, linked in the name of the parish of which they are both part, but they are quite different in character. East Malling is traditionally an agricultural village, with a number of old buildings, particularly at the crossroads that mark the centre of the village, where the church cranes its tower above the flanking trees to keep a benevolent eye on the villagers.

East Malling residents share, to some extent, in the papermaking economy of its neighbour, Larkfield, but its own contribution to the life of the county is the East Malling Research Station, known to fruit growers all over the world. The administrative headquarters of the Station is Bradbourne, the very fine eighteenth-century manor house of the Twisden family (whose Sir Roger, when he was a High Court Judge, imprisoned John Bunyon, author of Pilgrim's Progress) and the house is noted for some of the finest period brickwork in England. But modernity has claimed its share of the East Malling environs as well, and a very large estate, complete with schools, has been developed at Clare Park. Today, the village is well within the Kentish commuter belt.

Village greens are not particularly common in this land-hungry part of Kent, but Ditton, just south of the A20 has one. This is another of the villages just outside Maidstone that has grown rapidly in modern times, but there are still several architectural attractions to be found here, including the half-timbered former rectory, Stream Cottage, just behind Ditton Ford, and the old Mill House.

There is probably no village in all Kent that has been more often photographed and painted than Aylesford, and particularly that part of the village that clusters around the northern end of the old bridge across the river Medway.

Aylesford is, indeed, very old as a village of importance, mainly because it has been a river crossing for many centuries and history crowds upon itself in and around the village. It was here that Hengist and Horsa defeated the Britons in a great fifth-century battle, and made the way clear for the creation of the English nation. But Aylesford was important long before that even.

Outside the village, but within the parish, is Kit's Coty, Kent's 'little Stonehenge' as it has (quite inaccurately) been called. It is in fact what remains of a prehistoric burial chamber, from the huge stones of which the earth has been eroded so that they stand up clear of the ground.

Near the parish church, is the site of an Iron Age cemetery where Bronze Age relics have also been found, and the Romans knew Aylesford, too.

It is, undeniably, a very picturesque village today, with its red brick and timbered houses crowding in on the narrow main street and, at one end, the Friars, an important Carmelite house since the Order was re-established here in 1949. Before that, this was the first Carmelite establishment in England after it was founded in 1242, and it remained a prominent centre of the Order right up to the Dissolution. Today, the village centre caters for many thousands of visitors every year, and there are tea-shops and antique shops alongside the pubs and the houses.

But never far away are the industries that the river Medway, navigable for quite large barges to Allington Lock and above, has encouraged. And where there are industries, there are homes

L

—Aylesford today is very much more than the few picturesque old buildings that spread out from one side of the bridge.

Part of Aylesford parish is taken up by the Royal British Legion Village on the Preston Hall estate—a village founded by the Legion after the First World War where disabled soldiers and their families could live and work in sheltered conditions. Today, the village workshops produce furniture and garden sheds and much more besides, all in competition with other commercial undertakings.

Other villages and hamlets in the Aylesford parish include Cossington, Pratling Street and Eccles.

Today Snodland offers very little incentive to the casual visitor to linger in its curiously town-like main street, which is the A228 to Rochester, with its tributaries of residential streets flanked with frankly unattractive terraces under a more or less permanent pall of fine dust from the local cement works.

It is all very different from the Snodland the Romans knew—although they wouldn't have known it by that name, anyway. Six hundred years ago, Snodland had something of a reputation for its vines and where the gas works is now was once the site of a Roman building. Snodland is one of the Medway Gap villages, and the twin preoccupations of industry all the way along the north end of the Gap are cement-making and quarrying. Probably, the Canterbury pilgrims crossed the Medway by ferry from below Snodland, at the point where now the river is full of small pleasure craft and water-skiers draw their impermanent patterns on the grey water during the summer.

Once across the river, the Pilgrims' next stop might well have been at Burham, from where the Pilgrims' Way is signposted to lead the walker eastwards along the Downs.

North-west of Burham the new Blue Bell Hill road climbs the hill out of Maidstone to join up with the M2 and the roads down the other side of the Downs into the Medway Towns. At the top of the hill is the little community of Blue Bell Hill, grouped alongside the road from the 'Upper Bell' public house. It is a roadside community in every sense, depending now just as it did in the days when the coaches dispensed with the extra horses at the hill top, upon the traffic using the hill.

Right on the very outskirts of Maidstone is the attractive little village of Boxley, nestling at the very foot of the Downs, and surrounded by open farm and parkland.

Boxley church has for its immediate neighbour Boxley Park, which surrounds Boxley House Country Club. The church lies back from the village main street at the end of a wide cul-de-sac with grass verges and metalled carriageways, and an old cobbled path leading down the middle, through the lychgate, and to the church entrance. Conveniently, immediately opposite the church is the old white-painted brick frontage of the 'King's Arms', flanked on both sides by attractive old cottages and farm buildings.

The medieval Boxley Abbey was famous (or is 'notorious' the better word?) for its two miraculous statues, one of Christ crucified, the other of St Rumwold. The first was something of a mechanical marvel, jointed in such a way that the monks could make it move in an almost lifelike manner. The second was so made that it could be lifted by clean-living worshippers, but not by others. Righteousness was measured by the attendant monks by the generosity of the pilgrim's offering to the shrine, and demonstrated to the rest of the congregation by the removal (or not) of the pin that held the statue down. The two statues between them did a great deal to ensure that the good monks of Boxley did not lack creature comforts, but they did nothing for the reputation of the monastic life before the Dissolution. When the monastery was demolished in 1538, the figure of Christ was publicly burned in London, but the other one, of St Rumwold, was lost and has never been found. All that remains of the Abbey today are a few crumbling stone walls and a very large tithe barn, prominent on the right of the A20(M) for traffic by-passing Maidstone on the way to London.

Boxley also boasts an attractive little stream that Tennyson used as the model and inspiration for his famous poem 'The Brook'.

On the other side of the A20(M) is the almost wholly estate-type residential area of Allington, in which is Allington Castle, right down by the river Medway and now owned by and occupied by Carmelite monks as a place for retreats and conferences. Most of the castle dates from the fortifications of the original house on the site by Sir Stephen of Penchester in the late thirteenth century. It was subsequently owned by the Cobhams, Sir Henry Wyatt and his son, Sir Thomas Wyatt who was born at Allington and who is remembered best today by the hotel named after him which stands alongside the London Road, just out of Maidstone.

# 8

## *Romney Marsh*

NOBODY ever writes about Romney Marsh without quoting the *Ingoldsby Legend* passage: "The world, according to the best geographers, is divided into Europe, Asia, Africa, America and Romney Marsh. In this last named, and fifth, quarter of the globe, a witch may still be discovered in stormy seasons, careering on her broomstick over Dymchurch Wall." I certainly would not want to be the first to break such a well-established tradition and omit that quotation now. Neither would I want to suggest that there is not some element of truth in it, even today. I could not vouch for the careering witch. But as a man who knows the Marsh quite well, yet could never be more than a stranger there by reason of not having been born there of parents whose parents were also born there, I can vouch for the individuality of Romney Marsh.

Visitors notice it almost at once. Its location, on the very rim of the English realm, and its topographical characteristics, have isolated its hardy residents from the nation's law-givers and law-enforcers since very early on, right up to the last century—and indeed, although they are rather less blatant about it now, to this very day.

The men of Romney Marsh have been governing themselves for so long that even today they still tend to resent outside interference in what they regard as their own affairs. The Marsh covers one-twentieth of the county of Kent and until the last few years it had its own unique and very ancient local government, the Lords of the Level.

The region stretches from Hythe to the Sussex border town of Rye, and from Dungeness inland to Tenterden: about 50,000 acres in all. Really, only about 24,000 acres of that is properly Romney Marsh, and that is the land north-east of the Rhee wall, an early attempt at land reclamation by building a bank with a double ditch from Appledore to Romney. The rest of the area commonly included under the Romney Marsh label includes Walland and Denge Marshes and Guldeford level (about 22,600 acres altogether.)

Even less entitled to be included in the Marsh territory is the Isle of Oxney, west of the river Rother. Once this really was an island, rising up out of the sea from which the Marsh was won. It still has all the characteristics of an island, with land of a very high quality indeed rising up out of the flat surrounding pasture-lands to a significantly greater height, so that it can be seen even now to be an outcrop of the generally higher land beyond Small-hythe and Newenden. Yet visitors and outsiders might be for-given—at least by another outside like myself, if not by the Marshmen—for supposing that the Isle of Oxney is all part of the same geographical entity we call Romney Marsh.

The Marsh is not only often incorrectly labelled; it is also ill-named today for, far from being in any sense 'marshland', it is a well-drained area famous for the rich pastures on which have flourished for centuries the even more famous Romney Marsh breed of sheep. Incidentally, the sheep are responsible for a local whimsicallity unique to Romney Marsh where, it is said, there are a lot of real good lookers. There are, too: 'looker' is the Marsh word for shepherd or sheep minder.

Much of the Marsh is protected for its great landscape value, and some of it it is of special scientific interest for the unique wild life that flourishes there. The sea is kept at bay by a system of walls and embankments, but man cannot claim all the credit for the reclamation of this fertile wedge of land. A shingle bank built up which prevented the silt from the rivers Rother, Brede and Tillingham from flowing into the sea as they once did. This led to the change in the Rother's course, so that it empties into the English Channel at Rye, now. The original course can still be traced between Hammonds Corner and Old Romney. The great mass of shingle which the waves and the currents built up at Dungeness is still growing eastwards today.

The men of the Marsh trace their ancestry back to the early Britons. The Romans knew the area well, and after them the Saxons had to learn to share the good grazing with their Norman conquerors. It was probably not such an uneasy neighbourliness as in some other parts of England. Even then, the fierce individuality of the Romney Marsh natives would have prompted them to ignore as much as possible the newcomers who, in any case, exercised a delegated, more than direct, control over so wild and inhospitable an area. Besides, every settler on Romney Marsh has always had to sink his differences with his neighbours there into the common need to keep at bay the common predator, the sea.

It was the Romans who built Dymchurch wall, the great bank that still forms the first real line of defence against the sea. The Saxons built the Rhee wall from Romney to Appledore and Rye. But for all his ingenuity, man has not always won the ages-long battle. In the thirteenth century a forty-year period of storms so disturbed the whole area that the river Rother foresook its course across the marsh to find the sea at Romney, and created a new channel for itself through Rye. That change of course also changed the course of history for Romney, which declined almost overnight from being a major port to a country village, its harbour completely silted up.

The Marsh is probably less densely populated today than it once was. Every village has a church, and the parish churches of Romney Marsh form a very fine collection, mostly Norman and Early English. But there are the ruins of several more churches, too, suggesting that the medieval centuries, when the Abbeys of

Canterbury owned nearly all the Romney Marsh land, were times of less scattered communities than we find there today.

One of the most distinctive features of man's sojourn on the Marsh is the road—originally a great paved route—which the Romans built from Canterbury (their Durovernum) all the way to Lympne known to them as Portus Lemanis). The road is still there today: straight as a motorway, wide enough for the traffic it carries along most of its length, and more attractive than most of today's highways.

The Saxon Rhee wall added several thousands of acres to the Saxon kingdom of Merscwari and later, in King Alfred's days, the whole area was a favourite raiding-ground of the marauding Danes, who swept up the Rother in their long ships throughout the period from about 834 to 893, and they helped to form that characteristic guardedness of the natives, who became accustomed to going to their work each day fully armed in readiness for a surprise raid by the northern pirates.

No doubt they argued that if the Danes were going to come and push them about, there was no reason why they shouldn't push others about a bit, too, although the flourishing local sideline to the agricultural economy which involved luring vessels in the Channel on to the dangerous coastline with decoy beacons and then plundering them of their cargoes went on long after the Norsemen's raids ended.

The Marshmen also made salt, collecting sea-water in coastal 'pans' which allowed the water to evaporate, leaving behind the salt for collection and marketing.

In the Middle Ages the men of the Marsh were known for two characteristics: they had the reputation of being thoroughly truculent, and good actors. The first trait led to fights with visiting fishermen and sailors and on at least one occasion led to a full scale battle at Romney with a group of Yarmouth boatmen. The second characteristic carried the fame of the Romney Marsh miracle plays all over the Marsh, culminating in the annual Romney Passion Play which became an event of national renown.

The plays were unusual for the period in that they had women actors from at least as early as 1463.

At this period, the Marsh belonged almost wholly to the church—most of it to the two great abbeys of Canterbury—and this remained true up to the Dissolution.

The independence of the Marshmen sprang from two sources. First was the remoteness and inhospitable nature of their homeland. It was often very much easier (not to say safer) and a lot less trouble generally to allow the Marshmen to get away with fairly minor infringements of the law of the land than to try to enforce it. For example, both Lydd and Brockland held illegal markets (that is to say, they had no Royal permission to hold markets), and got away with it for many years before they were finally called to order.

But at least as important was the protection given to the Marshmen by their special and unique relationship with the Cinque Ports Federation; that rather remarkable organization of the main Channel coast ports from Sandwich in Kent to Hastings in Sussex. It was to the Ports that all England looked for protection in the narrow and vulnerable Channel that separated the country from the unfriendly neighbours on the European mainland. There was, therefore, little to be gained and a great deal at risk if the Portsmen and their Marshland allies were antagonized. They could afford, therefore, to show a certain disdain for any outside attempt at interference with their own unique system of local government —the first in the country. This was only true for any one town or village, of course, as long as it stayed close to the rest of the Federation members; it was very much a case of all for one and one for all, and this contributed considerably to the very great strength of the Cinque Ports as an autonomous organization.

In addition, Romney Marsh had the ever present danger of flooding to contend with—a danger that could become imminent at very short notice. When that happened, the residents could not wait while decisions were taken far off, nor for help to arrive, if it was needed, after those decisions were reached. There had to be organized action immediately. So the Marsh created its own system of local organization for such emergencies, and thus that second unique body of local government, the Lords of the Level, came into existence in the days of Edward IV.

The Lords consisted of a bailiff and twenty-three jurats, and gradually this body accrued very wide powers to maintain the fight against the sea. It levied its own tax, which took precedence over the Official Receiver in Bankruptcy, and the Lords could also take sand and soil without question from any landowner to repair the sea wall. In 1950, the jurats were elected for the last time, to be superseded, after four hundred years by the 1950 Justices of the Peace Act.

By the eighteenth century most of the Marshmen were engaged in smuggling in one way or another. Wool and weapons were smuggled out of the country to France, and brandy, silks and lace were brought back on the return journey by the Owlers who relied heavily upon their intimate knowledge of the intricate Marshland topography to keep the Revenue men at arm's length. Those were lawless and sometimes bloody days however they were romanticized later by authors like Russell Thorndyke, creator of the infamous Dr Syn.

During the Napoleonic wars, seventy-four Martello towers were built from Folkestone to Eastbourne, several of which are still to be seen today, and this first line of defence was backed up by the Royal Military Canal from Rye to Hythe, built in 1804. Another unique feature that crosses the Marsh is the famous 'little railway', the Romney, Hythe and Dymchurch railway, known everywhere as the world's smallest public railway.

In twentieth-century England, Romney Marsh retains its air of remoteness and indifference to the changes the years bring to the rest of the county or to the country. There are no incentives for the big 'juggernaut' lorries to trundle over its roads and the very high quality of the land for agricultural purposes offers a good deal of protection against any but the most strictly controlled development. But, in any case, developers do not crowd forward with applications to build here and the whole region still has to-day a close-to-nature look about the wide open pasture-land laced with dykes and gnarled old willows that have been stunted and bowed by the practically ceaseless wind that has tested their endurance for centuries.

It is a remote, withdrawn region where even the sun never seems to want to linger long, and yet it has a fascination that is as un-deniable as it is inexplicable.

Probably the most likely approach road for visitors to the Marsh is from the north. There are no really major roads across the Marsh itself. The nearest thing to a Romney Marsh highway is, I suppose the B2070 which runs south and east from Ashford through Orlestone and Ham Street to New Romney.

Orlestone, although it is outside the former Romney Marsh rural district (which disappeared under local government reorganization in 1947) is partly in the liberty of Romney Marsh and partly the Hundred of Ham in the lathe of Shepway. Nevertheless I shall regard it as the doorstep to the Marsh because it looks like part of the Marsh.

East of Orlestone, the B2067 strikes out for Hythe along a line just north of the Royal Military Canal. This route takes the traveller through Ruckinge, a little village on high ground on the borders of the Marsh and, like Orlestone, partly in the liberty of the Romney Marsh.

Ruckinge looks an unlikely village to have been the birthplace of the steam traction engines of Thos. Aveling in the 1860s, but the village sign confirms that it was by incorporating part of a steam roller in its design. The village church, which stands just aside from the road, displays an original Norman south doorway to go with its heavy-looking Norman tower. The Canal passes through the southern part of Ruckinge parish, much of which is woodland, and from the top of Ash Hill there is a fine view over the Marsh between Lympne and Fairlight.

Going out of Ruckinge towards neighbouring Bilsington, the

road is lined on the left with a queue of old farming machinery in a field.

Continuing along into Bilsington, this attractive little village stands on the side of a hill that slopes down to the Romney Marsh proper. Part of the parish stretches into the Levels of the Marsh, across the Royal Military Canal. The hall and undercroft of the old Bilsington Priory which was founded in 1253 and served as a lodging for the Archbishop of Canterbury when he visited the Marsh, remain just north of the village, adjoining the more modern Priory which is a private home. The original Priory of Austin Canons at Bilsington became Crown property at the time of the dissolution and eventually became a farmhouse. The priory estate was at one time the property of Sir William Cosway who, although he never did take up residence in the village, took a very keen interest in it and in the well-being of his labourers, and built a school for the children to be educated there. Sir William was killed in London when the Brighton coach in which he was travelling overturned, and the people of Ruckinge built as his memorial a 52-foot high obelisk. It is there today, crumbling in an open field, where it serves to arouse the curiosity of passers-by who do not know its history. It is, in fact, quite near the church of SS Peter and Paul, Bilsington, which dates from the thirteenth century and stands on a ridge overlooking the Marsh. From the churchyard there is a view out to the English Channel, and to the left there rises the cliff which, before the sea receded, was the old Channel coastline.

Just down the road is Bonnington. At the time of the Domesday Survey it was called Bonintone or Bunningtun, which is not important except to demonstrate that it is a very old-established settlement. In 1308 it was part of the property of the Knight's Templar and at Bonnington Corner, on the village green, there is an ancient tree known as the Law-Day Oak, under which the Leet Court once sat to hear and judge local cases.

An interesting reminder of times past is the name of a field just south-east of Bonnington Bridge. It is called Coal Wharf, and it was

to this point that Rye sailing barges once brought coal up the river
Rother to the Royal Military Canal. Bonnington has another claim
to fame, though: its parish church, the oldest of the Romney
Marsh churches, is the only one in Kent dedicated to St Rumwold.
It is said to stand on the site of a church first built there in 796.
St Rumwold was the three-day saint, born able to preach a sermon
before he died, three days old, and it was his 'miraculous' image
at Boxley Abbey near Maidstone that so scandalized reformists
of the sixteenth century, and the final fate of which remains unknown today.

To find Aldington, the traveller along the B2067 would have to
turn back on himself. The view from the village out across the
Marsh and the Channel is worth the slight detour, however. There
is an air of well-being about the little cluster of houses and the
pub—'The Good Intent'—and one gets the feeling that the old
houses have been lucky enough to have been appreciated and well-
maintained by successive owners. Aldington Knoll was the site of a
Roman beacon, and a Roman road from Clap Hill, just past Aldington Corner, leads through Broad Oak and South Stour to Chees-
man's Green. A number of Roman remains have been unearthed
between the Knoll and the village. The famous sixteenth-century
Dutch scholar Desiderius Erasmus was a rector of the church of
St Martin at Aldington; so was Thomas Lineacre, the English
scholar who taught Greek to Sir Thomas More and founded the
Royal College of Physicians.

The village found itself thrust into the centre of gossip
throughout Kent and indeed further afield when Elizabeth Barton,
called The Holy Maid of Kent, lived as a servant at the Archbishop's house there. Poor Elizabeth; she suffered from fits, during
which she was apparently able to prophesy and perform miracles
which would probably have earned her some notoriety but no
great harm if she had not allowed her gifts to trespass upon the
intended divorce of King Henry VIII from Catherine of Aragon.
Elizabeth foretold that if the divorce went ahead, the king would
lose this throne. In the politics of the time, that was accounted

treason and the unhappy girl was executed at Tyburn, although it seems that she was probably the ignorant dupe of local opponents of the Royal divorce, persuaded to voice views they shrank from broadcasting themselves.

From Aldington Corner past Stonestreet Green towards Smeeth, there is a bridge over the East Stour river at Evegate Mill, and a tributary of the river flows along the parish boundary and the edge of Backhouse Wood, through Hogben Farm and across the road at Aldington. The little church of St Martin, Aldington (part Norman, with Perpendicular style tower) houses some very good carved oak, including several stalls with misericords, and an old brass dating from about 1470. The church was restored in 1875.

Lympne (which, I do assure you, is pronounced *Limm*) stands high on a hill overlooking Hythe and the Marsh proper; in fact, on what was once the cliff above the Roman harbour of Portus Lemanis. There has been a village here or near here since ancient times, and the name derives from the old river Limene. Studfall Castle is the remains of the Roman fortress that guarded the port. Henry V built much of the Lympne Castle that remains to be seen today, and it was once the home of the Archbishop of Canterbury. The remains include the Square Tower, probably a Roman watch tower, and there was a Norman Hall before the Great Hall and Great Tower were built after 1360. Most of what remains today is unrestored fourteenth-century work.

Lympne was, like so many of the villages in and around Romney Marsh, a smuggling stronghold. There are a number of tales still told of those 'good old days'; often the same story is told as though it took place in several different villages. But Lympne Castle became the last home of a four-poster bed, featured in one tale as the hiding place for contraband gold which was pushed under the mattress by unbidden night visitors to the home of the doubtless terrified occupants of the bed.

Today, the village remembers its World War II airport, now Ashford Airport, from where operate service and charter flights to the Continent. It is actually the oldest service airfield in England, having been an RFC (Royal Flying Corps) and then an RAF station before it was 'demobbed'. It was from this field that Amy Johnson made her historic and record-breaking flight to Cape Town in 1932.

From Lympne, the traveller can choose: on to join the A261, which is the spur off the A20 into Hythe; or south, say to New-church.

A thoroughly typical Marshland village in a typically Marshland parish—that is Newchurch. The church there is by no means new; dedicated to SS Peter and Paul, it was built in the thirteenth century and enlarged during the fourteenth century. Early in this present century, restoration work was carried out and a remarkably vigorous wooden carving of a head with an apple clenched be-tween bared teeth was moved from the roof and is now in the South Chapel.

The parish is one of isolated farms, narrow lanes, dykes flanked by clumps of dispirited willows, and very little evidence that the twentieth century has ever found its way into this particular corner of Kent. Even the village has the appearance of being more a collection of farm buildings than of houses, yet the church is one of the largest on Romney Marsh—about the only hint that this was once the centre of the Hundred of Kent and deserved a very full entry in the Domesday Book, although there was no church there then.

East of Newchurch is Burmarsh, which stands behind Dym-church, moated by scores of dykes and drainage channels web-bing the pasturelands in which it stands—not as much pasture-land as there once was hereabouts, for much of the land is now cultivated. The village is just a cluster of old cottages and a council housing estate, quiet and isolated, with a nearby twelfth-century church. The name of the place is said to derive from the fact that this was once the area of the marsh that belonged to the burgesses of Canterbury.

Its nearest neighbours include the hamlet of Donkey Street and two settlements about which virtually nothing is known, but which once had their own churches, Orgarswick and Eastbridge. Orgarswick church has completely disappeared, and the site is marked today by a simple stone cross, but the ruins of Eastbridge church can still be traced.

Is Dymchurch a village any more? Not really. Nor is there much of the distinctive Marshland character to be seen in what has become a popular seaside resort, hemmed about with chalets and caravans and amusement areas and gift shops. None of these look out on to the sea because the sea wall—the modern successor of the original Roman Dymchurch wall that first began to push back the sea from this part of Kent. But Dymchurch has long been the 'capital' of the Marsh and the New Hall ('new' in 1580 and only then because it replaced a much older hall that was destroyed by fire) was the old meeting place of the Lords of the Level. Now it houses a small museum.

South again, through Blackmanstone, St Mary in the Marsh stands aloof from the holiday resort of St Mary's Bay, itself a village, but a modern one providing a halt for the famous Little Railway.

St Mary's Bay is a crescent of groyne-striped sand backed by a large holiday camp and all the associated amenities of shopping centre, church hall, pubs, and so on. There is a modern church, built in 1938. The beach is very safe, so that it is popular with parents of young children, as well as with fishermen and water sportsmen. When the beach palls, there is a playing field with a children's corner, and the village's ample car parking space makes it something of a mecca to holidaymakers—and something of an oddity as a neighbour for the reserve and isolation that is the much more general characteristic of the Marsh.

St Mary in the Marsh is the only other community of any size at all in the parish of the same name, and that is no more than a small hamlet today. Yet it, too, claims its share of history's note by having contrived to be the last resting place of E. Nesbit, writer of children's poems and stories, who died at St Mary's Bay in 1924.

Ivychurch is just about in the centre of the old Romney Marsh rural district, half way along the B2070 between Ham Street and New Romney. The parish stretches across the line of the Saxon Rhee Wall, which is now the Rye to New Romney road, and reaches across Walland Marsh to the very edge of Kent itself, where the county boundary is defined by the ancient Kent Ditch.

Ivychurch village stands at the north-eastern end of the parish the whole of which is typical Marsh country: level grazing land crossed by a network of small watercourses and ditches with lonely-looking farm buildings grouped at the ends of banked tracks above the Marsh. The village itself is very small; no more than a few cottages huddling together for shelter against the notorious Marsh winds that whip along the road, as though glad to find a purpose in life after the restless search across the flat fields. There is a pub, and St George's church which was once known as the 'Cathedral of the Marshes' and which had to be repaired after it was damaged by flying bombs during the Second World War. It is a big impressive-looking church, made massive with stepped buttresses and castellations, and like many another Marsh church, it shared in the local smuggling industry as a cache for contraband. It has been struck by lightning and it has been pressed into the service of Cromwellian cavalrymen as stables for their horses—one thing the Marsh churches can all claim is that they have shared very fully in the life of the local communities they have served through the years.

Off the B2070 is the B2081 which runs down through Brenzett Green and Brenzett to the apex of the dog-leg route of the A259 Romney–Rye road. There isn't very much to Brenzett, apart from the inevitable pub and St Eanswith's church. St Eanswith earned distinction among the saints by founding the first nunnery in all England. And although they left no long-lasting impression upon the village, it was to Branzett that the Romney Marsh supporters of Wat Tyler's rebellion in 1381 brought their pitchforks and billhooks in readiness for the brave but abortive march upon London.

The most westerly parish of the old Romney Marsh rural district was Snargate, where a mere handful of cottagers on the very edge of the flatlands can boast a quite large as well as very old church, St Dunstan's. Its embattled tower has a peal of three bells and a part of the aisle was once sealed off and used as a hideout for smugglers.

Richard Barham was once Rector of the church, in 1817, when he was 28. Born in Canterbury in 1788, he went on to become a canon of St Paul's Cathedral, but his personal toehold in history was made for him by his famous *Ingoldsby Legends*, rhymed verses written under the pen-name of Thomas Ingoldsby. *The Legends* were not his only venture into literary life—and they were not, in fact, written during his incumbency at Snargate—but they are the only work of that author that live on after him.

Where the road joins the A259, the choice is between forking left to Old Romney or right to Brookland. Brookland is the village that visitors always remember for St Augustine's church there because it has a unique detached timber belfry with a conical cap. It stands at the roadside, tiered in oak and tile, like a gigantic candle snuffer and must surely be the most-photographed feature of the whole of Romney Marsh. Naturally, there is a legend about why the bell-tower stands on its own alongside instead of, as is more usual, on top of the church. The story is that at one time the morals of the people of Brookland became very lax. People were living together without the benefit of church weddings! But then, one day, a young couple broke with the local custom and went to the church to ask the vicar to marry them. The shock (so the tale is told) was too much for the old church. The steeple toppled off the church and landed on the ground alongside, where it has been ever since, a memorial to the return to grace of the (now) good people of Brookland. You don't have to believe a word of it, but it is probably a lot more entertaining than the truth which, in any case, seems to have been blown from man's memory by the Marshlands winds.

Old Romney stands by the main road from Rye to New Romney. It is no more than a hamlet—a sad come-down from the days when it was a sea port of some importance with a flourishing trade. It is difficult for anyone standing in the village today to believe that a once important waterway reached right up to the town quay, but then, of course, it was a very long time ago. Even by 1377 the old part had fallen into much the same relative prominence it has today, so that Old Romney has had plenty of time to forget its good old days.

The church is both interesting and rarely picturesque, standing as it does aloof from the village in a field, with one solitary old yew tree to keep it company. Dedicated to St Clement, it has a fine timber roof with rare kingposts, and an eighteenth-century Minstrel's Gallery. Part of an early thirteenth-century painting in a rose design was uncovered in the chancel early in 1960.

If Romney Marsh were truly the fifth continent, then Dungeness might almost claim to be yet another, and sixth, continent for, although it is undeniably part of the Romney Marsh region, it is quite different in character from all the rest. It thrusts out into the Channel, an expanse of barren featureless shingle that bores the casual visitor with its emptiness and sends naturalists into ecstasies. It is an ideal spot for bird-watching and there is a Royal Society for the Protection of Birds reserve there. Practically its only other features are the huge piles of the Dungeness Power Station buildings, and the old lighthouse, inland now, with its more slender more modern-looking successor out on the new shoreline. There was a lighthouse at Dungeness in 1615—a tower with a beacon burning on the top. Since then, there has been a succession of new structures, always trying to keep pace with the receding shoreline, as the shingle continually builds up and changes the shape of this completely fascinating outpost of the Romney Marsh.

Returning inland, one might wonder not that few people ever find the little hamlet of Fairfield, on the Appledore–Brookland road, but that anyone does. Yet, like so many of the apparently inconsequential settlements on the Marsh, Fairfield has its church —a lonely little building at the end of a causeway above the marsh. Before the causeway was built, the church was periodically isolated on its knoll by floodwater and parishioners could only reach it by boat. It is said to be one of the oldest churches in England—a claim attributed to so many churches that it is of very little value—but it was built during the fourteenth century and rebuilt four hundred years after that, and restored in 1913. Services are still held there. The squat little wooden tower has three bells, recast from the fourteenth-century originals,; the original plaster between the timber framing is now replaced with bricks; and inside there are box pews and a three-deck pulpit. The church is dedicated to St Thomas à Becket, who owned land here. It is kept locked, but the key can be borrowed from the nearby Beckets Farm.

Littlestone-on-Sea can reasonably be included among the villages of Romney Marsh, although it is actually within the boundaries of what was, before the 1974 local government reorganization, New Romney borough. First developed in about 1816, it is now a busy and popular resort based upon the holiday camp site there. A mile further along the road to Dungeness is the twin resort of Greatstone-on-Sea.

In Roman times, Romney was an island, and the sea made coastal towns of villages that are today many miles inland: towns like Woodchurch, Appledore, Smallhythe, and Newenden. Wittersham was on what really was, then, the island of Oxney, and the little village of Ebony was an island, too. Two arms of the sea pincered round the islands towards Tenterden.

The picture was not very different in the Middle Ages, except that by then sandbanks had begun to enclose the inland sea and the Dymchurch wall from Hythe to Romney and the Rhee wall from Appledore to the Romney islet had reclaimed a great tract of marshland that already put Woodchurch and Lympne well inland. Lydd had grown up on a large island south of Romney, which was by this time part of the reclaimed land—of the Romney Marsh proper.

It is because of this build-up of sea-won land that the true Romney Marsh shares many of its topographical characteristic with the formerly inundated land, reaching into the Weald and lapping up to the outskirts of Tenterden.

Smallhythe, for instance, borders on the Reading Sewer—which is not as bad as it sounds because in this part of the country they still give the word 'sewer' its old meaning of watercourse for draining marshland. Reading Sewer follows the original north channel of the river Rother, which once made Smallhythe the thriving port for the nearby town of Tenterden. Now, it is a small, roadside hamlet with just one claim on the visitors' interest in Smallhythe Place, a half-timbered yeoman's house dating from 1480 and originally the residence of the port officer. Then, it was the Port House and there is still to be traced in the garden a slip repair dock that went out of use after the channel silted up and left Smallhythe high, dry and landlocked. What really made it famous, though, was its good fortune to be chosen as the home of the actress Dame Ellen Terry, who bought it in 1899 and lived there until she died in 1928. Now it is a museum full of relics of the actress herself and of other theatrical celebrities. It is owned by the National Trust and in the grounds is the Barn Theatre. Smallhythe's other claim to fame rests in the nearby Bulleign Farm, which was once owned by the family of Anne Boleyn.

Ebony has actually moved. The original island of Ebony is now Chapel Bank, and the church that once stood there has now been moved to the hamlet of Reading Street which is within the boundaries of the old borough of Tenterden.

Until as recently as 1932 the visitor to the Isle of Oxney who wanted to cross the Ferry Bridge had to pay a toll, and a board outside the Ferry Inn remains to remind today's travellers that it cost 1d. to take a pig across, 3d. for a score of lambs, and so on.

The Isle of Oxney is not all low-lying and the western higher part offers a site for the village of Wittersham, on the main Tenterden to Rye road. This was once the home of the Hon. Alfred Lyttelton, cricketer and politician—and remembered in that order, if you please!

Woodchurch is another of those Marshland satellites. Well inland today, it is a village that has attracted some new development
a little aloof from the village centre, which remains a very
attractive spot around a quite large village green. In the centre of
the village is Townland, the former (1135) Manor of Thunlande.
The church includes among its features two very fine brasses, one
of Nicholas de Gore, priest in 1320, which is the third oldest
in Kent.

Woodchurch has one of Kent's vanishing windmills, one of a
pair. One was damaged in a gale and pulled down, but the other
has been cared for by the villagers and remains a distinctive landmark to be seen from many miles away.

I certainly would not take issue with anyone who asserted that
Appledore is not part of Romney Marsh. It is, for sure, on the
'wrong' side of the Royal Military Canal, if only just, and equally
certainly it has a look of the Weald about it. On the other hand,
its history has been for centuries more closely linked with the
Marsh than with any other region. Once there were shipyards at
Appledore, even though today it is about nine miles from the sea,
left without its river when that great storm of 1287 took it away
and left it to nod off during the succeeding centuries into one of
south-east Kent's most attractive villages, remote, with poor
access, yet with an unusually wide main street which leads up
from the Canal, past the small square block of the Old Watch
House. This is the picturesque end of the village, where the
approach road widens into a small square surrounded by the ivy-
clad Red Lion hotel in front of the church, the old blacksmith's
shop, and The Swan Hotel. The Swan introduced an intriguing
little mystery into village lore a few years ago when a new licen-
see moved in and, during rebuilding work, discovered a wooden
chair with a silver engraved plate ascribing the chair to 'Sheikh
Mbaruk Bin Raschid Mwele' and dated August 1895. The tale was
told that a British naval squadron was despatched to Nweli in
East Africa with a punitive expedition commanded by General
Sir Lloyd William Mathews. But the wily sheikh had escaped and

was never heard of again, leaving the mystery of how his chair came to be found in a Kent inn.

At the other end of Appledore there has been some quite recent development, including a small council estate, and the village has become popular as a place of retirement.

Another of the borderland villages is Kenardington, which also lies on the edge of the Royal Military Canal. It is not comparable with Appledore in any other respect, though: just a few cottages and a massive-towered church with an outside stair turret characteristic of several of the thirteenth-century Marsh churches.

Kenardington Manor dates from, probably, the end of the fifteenth century, but it is on the site of an earlier Norman— possibly Saxon—manor house. It was, in fact, one of three assigned by William the Conqueror to provide an income for the Custodian of Dover Castle. Near the church there are the remains of an earthworks system said to have been raised by King Alfred as protection against the Danes. In the ninth century, the raiders landed at Appledore, but were prevented from pushing inland and occupying much more of this part of Kent by the fighting farmers of Kenardington.

Almost equally distant from Ashford and New Romney, and on the high ground that rises up from the Marsh, is Warehorn, a small village with an attractive little village green and some old buildings that include the Woolpack Inn—a reminder of the days when wool was a staple of the smuggling industry that flourished throughout the wilder and more remote parts of Kent. Author of the *Ingoldsby Legends*, the Reverend Richard Barham, was curate of Warehorn until 1821.

A real border village is Newenden, on a ridge of high ground between the river Rother and the Hexden Channel. On the east, the Rother Levels frequently flood, but there is little to remind resident or visitor that there was a time when the village's position at the end of the wide river Rother estuary made it into a strategic defence post against invaders with their piratical eyes on the Weald. As the estuary silted up and the water crept away, the threat receded with it, and left Newenden to dream of departed glory.

Stone-in-Oxney was well-known to the Romans, as is evidenced by the Mithraic altar, dated about third century, and carved with the Mithraic bull, which now stands in St Mary's church, but which was used before that for centuries as a mounting block outside the inn. The church also contains a 130-million-year-old relic—the fossilized bones of a dinosaur excavated from Stone quarry. The village has a small, compact centre which sends out tendrils along the main road in both directions, and there are three different groups of council houses. From the top of the old cliffs, there are magnificent views over the Rother valley into Sussex, across the marshes to the sea, and eastwards to the hills of Folkestone. The church is one of several buildings of architectural or historic interest in the village. Others include Rysings at the southern end of the main part of the village, parts of Churchlands Farm and Stone Green Farm. In the north, outside the village centre, Priory Farmhouse and nearby Chapel Cottage are also of special interest, and further north still, the group of buildings formed by the Ferry Inn (formerly the Isle of Oxney Inn) and its stables combine with adjoining Ferry Cottage and Myrtle Cottage into an attractive group.

# *Index*